MySQL Replication

MySQL Replication

An Administrator's Guide to Replication in MySQL

Russell J.T. Dyer

A Silent Killdeer Publishing (aslilentkilldeer.com)
New Orleans • Milan

MySQL Replication

Written by Russell J.T. Dyer.

Copyright © 2010 Russell J.T. Dyer.

All Rights Reserved. Except as permitted under the U.S. Copyright Act of 1976, no part of this publication may be reproduced, distributed, or transmitted in any form or by any means, or stored in a database or retrieval system, without the prior written permission of the author.

Although the publisher has tried to be careful in their part in the creation of this book, and the author has taken equal care for his part, neither the publisher nor the author assume responsibility for errors or omissions, nor do they assume responsibility for damages that might be caused from using or relying on information contained in this book.

This book contains several references to MySQL, a product of Sun Microsystems and Oracle Corporation, and references to products derived from MySQL. MySQL is a registered trade mark of Sun and Oracle.

The scanning, uploading and distributing of this book via the Internet or via any other means without the permission of the publisher or author is illegal and punishable by law. Please purchase only authorized electronic editions, and do not participate in or encourage electronic piracy of copyrighted materials.

A Silent Killdeer Publishing

Published by A Silent Killdeer Publishing, New Orleans, Louisiana, U.S.A. Visit our web site at http://asilentkilldeer.com or email us at inquiries@asilentkilldeer.com. Printed in the United States of America. Set in the Geneva font.

ISBN: 978-0-9831854-0-6

To my friend, Jerry Neumeyer who taught me that it's alright to be me and to do all the insane things I want to do in life—especially since I'm eventually going to die.

Table of Contents

Preface.. ix

Introduction.. 1

Part I: Understanding & Preparation..............................5
    Chapter 1: MySQL Replication Process........................7
    Chapter 2: Replication User Account......................... 29
    Chapter 3: Configuring Servers................................35

Part II: Priming & Starting.. 45
    Chapter 5: Alternative Copy Methods.......................53
    Chapter 6: Starting MySQL Replication...................... 61

Part III: Administration.. 71
    Chapter 7: Backups with Replication........................73
    Chapter 8: Restoring Backups...................................83
    Chapter 10: Load Balancing.....................................103

Appendixes... 109
    Appendix A: SQL Statements & Functions...............111
    Appendix B: MySQL Replication States.....................131
    Appendix C: MySQL Daemon & Utilities.....................149

Preface

MySQL is the most popular open source database system available. It's particularly useful and is used with public web sites which require a fast and stable database. So as to protect data and ensure uninterrupted service, many organizations use the replication feature of MySQL. However, replication is not covered in many books on MySQL. When it is addressed, most authors provide very little information on the topic. In the second edition of my book, *MySQL in a Nutshell* (O'Reilly 2008), I introduced a chapter solely on MySQL Replication. However, it wasn't enough. I wanted to expand on that text and to provide related information in a book dedicated to MySQL Replication. The result is this book.

It's my hope and goal that MySQL administrators who already know the basics of MySQL, can use this book to learn about MySQL Replication and that it will assist them in keeping it running or to get it running again when it inevitably stops.

Text Based and Operating Systems

Some people feel that graphical interfaces are faster. However, while a picture may be worth a thousand words, when you only want to say one word, why would you draw a picture. I don't like graphical user interfaces for controlling a server or MySQL Interfaces tend to change between versions and interfaces. Command-line utilities are very stable and their basic commands don't change usually. If you know how to configure a server at the command-line, it hardly matters what kind of server you're on. The only exception may be Windows servers. Any examples in this book which are executed within MySQL are universal. Any examples at the command-line are for Unix types of operating systems (e.g., Linux). I don't provide the Windows equivalent since I don't know them. I leave it up to the reader to make the necessary adjustments for his operating system.

Reading Suggestions

Assuming you are new to MySQL replication, you may find it most useful to read this book in sequential order, at least for the first two parts—although I suspect most readers will do well to skip Chapter 5, Alternative Copy Methods. Part III, Administration explains what to do once MySQL Replication is running. So you might delay reading the chapters that it contains for a while.

If you do read completely the first five or six chapters in order, you will notice some traits about my writing style for this book. One trait in particular that I would like to point out is my occasional redundancy. Any one chapter in this book will stand somewhat on its own. At the beginning of each chapter, especially the chapters in the first two parts, there is a recap of the steps the reader goes through in setting up on running replication. This is meant to help the reader reinforce what he has already read, as well as to to remind the reader where he is at this point. For readers who skip around in their reading of chapters, this style is to help them keep from getting lost. Besides the chapter openings, I also repeat information at key points in the text to remind the reader about elements of the replication process covered in the first chapter. It try to keep my redundancy to a minimum, but I think it is useful.

Typographical Conventions

In organizing this book, certain typographical conventions were used. Here is a list of the primary ones employed with examples of their typesettings:

- `Constant width text` is used for software commands and functions, file names and paths, as well as code examples. The same font style is used for SQL statements and functions, but with all capital letters.

- *Italic text* is used for web site and email addresses. It's also used for new terms when first introduced.

- `Constant width, italic text` is used to designate database, table, and column names and file names that are not determined by the user's preferences.

- Plain text of various font sizes are used for all other text throughout this book.

Scripts & Programs

All of the scripts and programs shown in the book can be found on the web for you to easily copy and modify for your own use. They can be found on the web at http://mysqlresources.com/books/mysql_replication/scripts/.

Acknowledgements

Thanks to my colleagues, Bogdan Kecman, Giuseppe Maxia, Jonas Sundin for reviewing this book for technical accuracy and for advice and other information critical to it's creation. Thanks to my old boss from MySQL AB, Ulf Sandberg for his support and encouragement over the past five years. Thanks also to my friend and co-worker, Rusty Osborne for her friendship and patience while working on this book and while I built my writing career. Finally, thanks to my girlfriend, Paola Caporale for her love.

About the Author

Russell Dyer is a writer and editor living in both New Orleans, U.S.A. and Milan, Italy. Besides novels and short stories, he has written and published books on software (e.g., *MySQL in a Nutshell,* O'Reilly Media, 2008). He has written hundreds of articles on software (his specialty being MySQL), travel and economics. See his web site for more information about him and his works: `http://russell.dyerhouse.com`

Introduction

One of the difficulties in maintaining a large and active MySQL database is making clean back-ups without having to shut down the MySQL server. Performing a back-up, though, while a server is running can slow down a system considerably. Additionally, back-ups made on active servers can result in inconsistent data because related tables may be changed while others are being copied. Taking down the server ensures consistency of data, but interrupts MySQL service to users. Sometimes this is necessary and unavoidable, but daily server outages for backing up data may be an unacceptable choice.

A simple alternative is to set up replication of MySQL so that one or more redundant servers maintain a consistent and continuous copy of the main MySQL server's databases. Then this redundant server can be shut down for back-ups while the main server continues serving the users.

Typically, setting up MySQL Replication is primarily a matter of configuring multiple servers so that the primary server where users submit their data changes, known in this context as a *master* server, houses the data and handles client requests. The master server logs all data changes locally to a binary log file. The master in turn informs another MySQL server (a *slave* server), which contains a copy of the master's databases, of any additions to its binary log. The slave in turn copies the pertinent SQL statements from the master to a binary log on its file system. It then executes locally these SQL statements, thus changing identically the data on its copy of the databases.

As a data back-up method, you can set up a separate server to be a slave and then once a day (or however often you prefer), turn off replication on the slave to make a clean back-up of the slave server's databases. When you're finished making the back-up, replication can then be restarted on the slave. The slave will then query automatically the master for changes to the master's data that the slave missed while it was offline.

There are other uses for replication. In particular, there's *load balancing*. Load balancing is the method of distributing user activities between multiple MySQL servers to increase performance. Otherwise, the system resources of one MySQL server may be over taxed and become sluggish. Load balancing is also useful in protecting against network and other system outages. If one MySQL server becomes inaccessible to users, user traffic can be redirected to other servers at different locations without loss of service.

As you may imagine, replication is an excellent feature. Best of all, it's built into the core of MySQL. It doesn't require you to buy or to install any additional software. You just set up physically at least one slave server and configure appropriately MySQL on both the master and slave servers to begin replication. To perform regular back-ups, it's only a matter of developing a script to stop routinely the replication process, make a back-up of the slave's data, and then restart replication. Setting up load balancing is much more involved, but it's possible to do with some configuring and programming.

To understand how to make replication efficient and robust in a particular environment, we'll look in detail at the steps that MySQL goes through to maintain a replicated server. The process is different depending on the version of MySQL your servers are using. This book applies primarily to version 4.0 or higher of MySQL. There were some significant improvements made in version 4.0 related to how replication activities are processed, making it much more dependable. Actually, although most of what is explained in this book will apply to version 4.0, it is written in consideration of version 5.1 of MySQL.

It is recommended that you always upgrade your servers if they are using an older version. There are many benefits to upgrading to version 5.1 of MySQL. Be careful, though: You should upgrade one release at a time, and use the same version of MySQL on both the master and all slave servers. Otherwise you may experience problems such as authentication between servers, incompatible table schemas, and other problems.

4, MySQL Replication

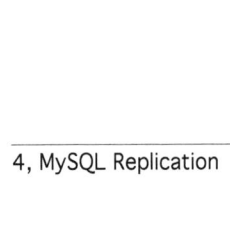

Part I
Understanding & Preparation

On the surface, replication in MySQL can seem fairly simple and straightforward. In many ways it is simple. However, unless you know what you're doing, trying to start replication can feel like trying to start an old car with manual transmission that either won't start or when it does, it bucks and dies when you're not paying attention: it can be very frustrating. There are no wizards or automated systems with MySQL Replication, and there isn't an OK button to click. It doesn't come with graphical displays to show you how your replication system is humming along, smoothly. Instead, it's up to you to know what to do, to monitor regularly the activities of all servers involved, and to know how to troubleshoot problems that will arise and resolve them without loss of services or data.

To be effective at starting and maintaining replication—especially without experiencing significant amounts of stress—you will need to understand MySQL Replication. You'll have to understand what is actually happening on the servers, where each server is in the replication process.

Since replication can involve the transferring of all of your MySQL data between servers over a network or even the internet, for proper security you should also understand what is involved in creating special user accounts and what privileges to assign these user accounts. Finally, before you can begin replication, you will need to configure the master and slave servers, properly. You will have to make sure that their individual configurations are complementary so as to maintain synchronization once replication begins. Basically, this part of the book is about preparing yourself and your servers for running MySQL Replication.

Chapter 1
MySQL Replication Process

In this chapter we'll go through the various steps of the MySQL Replication process. The master server has its set of tasks, while the slave does its job. It can be confusing since the process does not proceed as straightforward as one might suspect initially. To protect data from being lost in the process due to power failures, network problems, and other factors, all data is recorded multiple times in multiple locations, and each minor step of the process is noted. It's noted in surprisingly verbose ways. To help you follow along, I am a little verbose in the text of the chapter, especially by adding headings for each minor step described.

It is my hope that if you take your time in reading this chapter, when you're finished you will understand the complex process of MySQL Replication. I realize that it's plenty to absorb in so few pages. So I do expect that as you read through the subsequent chapters and begin to apply what you learn in this chapter, you will return to it to reread it. In fact, I imagine that this book and this chapter in particular will be the kind of text you will return to many times over many months or even years as you become comfortable with MySQL Replication.

What's Replicated & Where

When replication is running, SQL statements that change data are recorded in a binary log (`bin.000000`) on the master server as it executes them. Only SQL statements that change the data or the schema are logged. This includes data changing statements such as `INSERT`, `UPDATE`, and `DELETE`, and schema changing statements such as `CREATE TABLE`, `ALTER TABLE`, and `DROP TABLE`. It includes actions that effect data and schema that are executed from the `mysql` client, by applications (e.g., PHP web pages), and from the command-line by utilities such as `mysqladmin`. It does not include `SELECT` statements or any SQL statements that only query the server for information (e.g., `SHOW TABLES`).

Knowing What was Missed

Along with pertinent SQL statements, the master server records a log position identification number for each entry. The slave servers for their part will each note the position number of the last entry they received. This identifier will be used to determine which log entries the master should relay to the slave server or servers. This is necessary because slave servers may not always be able to receive consistently information from the master. For instance, an administrator might stop replication on the slave to make a back-up of the slave's databases. Besides maintenance activities, there may be times when the slave has difficulty staying connected to the master due to network problems. A slave may also fall behind in replicating simply because the master has a large number of updates in a short period of time, causing them to queue. Regardless of the reasons, when a slave reconnects minutes, hours, or even days later, with the position identification number of the last log entry it received, the slave can tell the master where it left off in its binary log. With this bit of information, the master can send the slave all of the subsequent entries it missed while it was disconnected. The master can do this even if the entries are contained in multiple log files due to the master's logs having been flushed one or more times in the interim.

Binary Log Example

To help you better understand the replication process, I've included—in this section especially, and throughout this book—sample excerpts from each type of replication log and index file. Knowing how to sift through logs will be useful when resolving server problems stemming not only from replication, but from corrupt or erroneously written data.

Here's an excerpt from a master binary log file:

Example 1.1: Master Binary Log

```
/usr/local/mysql/bin/mysqlbinlog \
   /var/log/mysql/bin.000007 \
   > /home/russell/binary_log.txt

tail --lines=14 /home/russell/binary_log.txt
# at 1999
```

Binary Log Example

```
#101120 9:53:27 server id 1 end_log_pos 2158  Query
thread_id=1391 exec_time=0 error_code=0
USE personal;
SET TIMESTAMP=1290264807;
CREATE TABLE contacts2 (contact_id INT AUTO_INCREMENT
KEY, name VARCHAR(50), telephone CHAR(15));

# at 2158
#101120  9:54:53 server id 1  end_log_pos 2186   Intvar
SET INSERT_ID=1;

# at 2186
#101120  9:54:53 server id 1 end_log_pos 2333  Query
thread_id=1391 exec_time=0 error_code=0
SET TIMESTAMP=1290264893;
INSERT INTO contacts2 (name, telephone) VALUES ('Rusty
Osborne', '001-504-838-1234');
```

As the first line shows, the command-line utility `mysqlbinlog` was used to read the contents of the server's binary log file. Note, the command-line entries here are bold-faced, while the log excerpts are not. The log file is in a binary format, so `mysqlbinlog` is provided with MySQL to make it possible for administrators to read the files. Because the log is extensive, I have redirected the results to a text file in the /home/russell directory using the shell's redirect operator (i.e., >). On the second command-line, I used the `tail` command to display the last fourteen lines of the text file generated, which in this case translates to the last three entries. You could instead pipe (i.e., |) the contents to `more` or `less` on a Linux or Unix type of system if you intend to scan only briefly the results. However, after you redirect the `mysqlbinlog` results of a binary log to a text file, the text file may be used to restore data on the master server to a specific point in time. Point-in-time recovery methods are an excellent recourse for restoring a particular range of data that you may have deleted inadvertently, or perhaps to restore a large amount of data that has been added since your last back up.

The Master Coughs

While the master is recording data in its binary log, the slave server, through an *I/O thread* (i.e., input/output thread), listens for communications from the master which will inform the slave of new entries in the master's binary log and of any changes to its data. The master does not transmit data unless requested by the slave. Nor does the slave continuously harass the master with inquiries as to whether there are new binary log entries. Instead, after the master has made an entry to its binary log, it looks to see whether any slaves are connected to the master and waiting for updates. The master then pokes the slave to let it know that an entry has been made to the master's binary log in case the slave is interested. It's then up to the slave to request the entries. Assuming the slave is eager and not otherwise occupied, it will ask the master to send entries starting from the position identification number of the last log file entry the slave processed.

Synchronizing Watches and All

Going back to the sample binary log excerpt I presented a couple of pages back and looking at each entry you will notice that each starts with the position identification number (e.g., 1999) that I keep mentioning. The second line of each entry provides the date (e.g., 101120 for

Synchronizing Watches and All

November 20, 2010), the time, and the replication server's identification number. This is followed by the position number expected for the next entry. This number is calculated from the number of bytes of text that the current entry required. It's a byte counter, not a simple numeric sequential counter. The rest of the entry provides stats on the thread which executed the SQL statement on the master. In some of the entries, a SET statement is provided with the TIMESTAMP variable so that when the binary log entry is used on the slave or maybe to restore data on the master, the date and time will be adjusted on the receiving server to match the date and time of the entry at the time the SQL statement was executed originally. The final line of each entry lists the SQL statement which was executed. Each SQL statement mentioned here (i.e., the SET TIMESTAMP, as well as the original SQL statements) are considered to be *events*.

Buried in the first entry of the excerpt you may have noticed that it begins with a USE statement. It's included in the binary log to ensure that the slave makes the subsequent changes to the correct database. Similarly, notice that the second entry sets the value of the variable, INSERT_ID in preparation for the INSERT statement that follows it. This ensures that the value to be used for the column (i.e., *contact_id* in this example) on the slave is the same as it was on the master. Nothing is left to chance or assumed, if possible. The slave's databases must be identical to the master's database in every way.

Keeping Track of Master Logs

As I alluded previously, the master server starts a new binary log file whenever the server is restarted or flushed. The master keeps track of the names of the binary log files in a simple text file (`bin.index`). When researching a problem with replication or trying to paste together a restoration, you may need to know about this file. An excerpt from a binary index file follows:

Example 1.2: Master Binary Index File

```
/var/log/mysql/bin.000001
/var/log/mysql/bin.000002
/var/log/mysql/bin.000003
/var/log/mysql/bin.000004
/var/log/mysql/bin.000005
/var/log/mysql/bin.000006
/var/log/mysql/bin.000007
```

This list of binary log files can also be obtained by executing the SHOW MASTER LOGS statement on the master. Notice that the list here includes the full path name of each binary log file in order, reflecting the order in which the files were created. The master appends each file path and name to the end of the index file as each log file is created. If a slave has been off-line for a several days, the master will search backwards through the files to find the file containing the position identification number given to it by the slave, unless the slave supplies the master with the name of the binary log file. It will then read that file from the entry following the specified position identification number to the end, followed by the subsequent files in order, sending SQL statements from each to the slave until the slave is current or disconnected. If the slave is disconnected before it can become current, the slave will make another request when it later reconnects with the new, last master log position identification number it received. It will persist in this way with the master until it has replicated fully the master's databases.

Encouraged Nagging

After the slave is current again, it will go back to waiting for another announcement from the master regarding changes to its binary log. The slave will make inquiries only when it receives another nudge from the master, or if quite a long time has gone by since it has heard from the master, or if it is disconnected temporarily. When a slave reconnects to the master after a disconnection, it makes inquiries to be sure it didn't miss anything while it was disconnected. If it sits idle for a long period, the slave's connection will time out, also causing it to reconnect and make inquires.

It is by this system of nudging, connecting, inquiring, and transmitting which slaves are able to stay current. It may seem like an excessive amount of unnecessary activities, but it's all done rapidly and the pokes back and forth are not a significant drain on resources since everything is done with simple and small transmissions.

Procrastinating

When the slave receives new changes from the master, the slave doesn't update its databases, directly. Direct application of changes was tried in with replication prior to MySQL 4.0. It was found to be too inflexible for managing heavy loads, especially if the slave's databases are also used to support user read requests (i.e., the slave is part of a load balancing scheme). Tables in the slave's replicated databases may be busy when the slave is attempting to update the data. A SELECT statement could be executed with the HIGH_PRIORITY flag, giving it priority over UPDATE and other SQL statements that change data and are not also entered specifically with the HIGH PRIORITY flag. In this case, the replication process would be delayed by user activities. On a busy server, the replication process could be delayed for several minutes. With this old method, if the master server crashed during a lengthy delay, it would mean the loss of many data changes of which the slave was not informed due to it waiting on access to a table on its own system.

By separating the recording of entries received from their execution, the slave is assured of getting all or almost all transactions up to the time that the master server crashes. It is asynchronous, but it's a much more dependable method than the one used in earlier versions of MySQL. With the current method, the slave appends changes to a file on its file system named, relay.000000.

Taking Notes

To help understand the process better and to help you to be able to resolve problems that slaves may have when replicating, it's useful to know how to read a slave's relay log file. An excerpt from a slave's relay log

Taking Notes

follows. It was generated with the utility, `mysqlbinlog` since the relay log is like a binary log, not in plain text format.

Example 1.3: Slave Relay Log

```
/*!40019 SET @@session.max_insert_delayed_threads=0*/;
/*!50003 SET
@OLD_COMPLETION_TYPE=@@COMPLETION_TYPE,COMPLETION_TYPE=0*/;

# at 4
#101118  3:18:40 server id 2  end_log_pos 98
   Start: binlog v 4, server v 5.1.41-log created 051118
3:18:40

# at 98
#700101  1:00:00 server id 1  end_log_pos 0 Rotate to
bin.000025 pos: 4

# at 135
#100819 11:40:57 server id 1  end_log_pos 98
   Start: binlog v 4, server v 5.1.41-log created 050819
11:40:57 at startup
ROLLBACK;

# at 949
#100819 11:54:49 server id 1  end_log_pos 952
    Query thread_id=10 exec_time=0 error_code=0
SET TIMESTAMP=1282211689;
CREATE TABLE prepare_test (id INTEGER NOT NULL, name
CHAR(64) NOT NULL);

# at 952
#100819 11:54:49 server id 1  end_log_pos 1072
    Query thread_id=10 exec_time=0 error_code=0
SET TIMESTAMP=1282211689;
INSERT INTO prepare_test VALUES ('0','zhzwDeLxLy8XYjqVM');
```

This log is like the master's binary log. Notice that the first entry mentions the server's identification number, 2, which is the slave. There are also some entries for server 1, the master. Remember, server identification numbers are arbitrary and set by the database administrator in the respective options files (i.e., `my.cnf` or `my.ini`, depending on your system). The first entries relate to log rotations on both servers. The last two are SQL statements relayed to the slave from the master.

A new relay log file is created when replication starts or restarts on the slave and when the logs are flushed (i.e., the FLUSH LOGS statement is executed). A new relay log file is also created when the current file reaches the maximum size as set in the `max_relay_log_size` variable when `mysqld` is started on the slave. The maximum size can also be limited by the `max_binlog_size` variable on the slave. If these variables are set to 0, there is no size limit placed on the relay log files. This is not recommended, though.

The Slave's Bookmarks

Once the slave has made note in its relay log of the SQL statements relayed to it by the master, it records the new position identification number in its master information file (`master.info`) on its file system in the data directory for MySQL—set with the `--datadir` option of `mysqld`. Here is an example of the content of a master information file on a slave server:

Example 1.4: Slave's master.info File

```
15
binary_log.000081
9748624
master_host
replicant
its_pwd
3306
60
0
```

The Slave's Bookmarks

This file is kept primarily so that the slave can remember its position in the master's binary log file even if the slave is rebooted, as well as the information necessary to reconnect to the master. Each line has a specific purpose:

- The first line contains the number of lines of data in the file itself. Although fewer than 15 lines are visible here, the actual file contains six blank lines at the end to make up for the rest.

- The second line above is the name of the last binary log file on the master from which the slave received entries. If the slave provides this binary log file name to the master, rather than just giving it the position number, it will help the master to respond faster to slave requests for new events in the master binary log.

- The third line shows the position identification number (i.e., `9748624`) in the master's binary log.

- The next few lines contain the master's host address, the replication user name, its password, and the port number (i.e., `3306`). Notice that the password is not encrypted and is stored in clear text. Therefore, be sure that this file, the `master.info` file is in a secure directory. You can determine the path for the file in the slave's configuration file, as discussed later in this chapter.

- The next to last line lists the number of attempts the slave should make when reconnecting to the master before stopping. In this case it shows, 60.

The Slave's Bookmarks

> The last line is 0 because the server from which this master information file came does not have the SSL feature enabled. If SSL was enabled on the slave and allowed on the master, there would be a value of 1 on this line. The line would also be followed by six more lines containing values related to SSL authentication, completing the fifteen lines anticipated on the first line. So, as the developers of MySQL decide that additional data related to the master should be stored in this file, more lines will be added and the first line will show a count other than 15. In fact, not long ago, before MySQL version 5.1.18, it used to say 14.

Instead of looking in this text file for information, you can use the SQL statement, SHOW SLAVE STATUS to get the same information. However, you can't get the replication user account's password from that SQL statement. You have to look in `master.info` file for it. If you want to make any changes to the data in this file, don't do it, directly. Instead, use the SQL statement, CHANGE MASTER TO for changing this data including the replication user account's password. See Appendix A for details on this SQL statement and others mentioned in this chapter.

Just as the `master.info` file on the slave is used to bookmark the slave's position in the master's binary log, the slave bookmarks it's position in its relay log. It notes their information in the `relay-log.info` file. Below is an example of its contents:

Example 1.5: Slave's relay-log.info File

```
/var/logs/relay.000006
28839226
```

The Slave's Bookmarks

```
binary_log.000081
57332181
```

The first line here contains the file path and name of the current relay log file on the slave. The second line contains the position of the last event in the relay log that the slave successfully executed. Next is the name of the master's binary log file from which this last successful event was read. The last item is the position in that master binary log file.

These last two lists of information may not always equal their equivalents in the `master.info` file. The `master.info` file's values relate to what was received and recorded in the relay log on the slave. The `relay-log.info` file notes on the master binary log relate to what was successful executed on the slave, taken from the relay log—the master log file name and position are just the corresponding bits of data related to those entries.

Slave Status

As mentioned above, the same information that can be found in the text files `master.info` and `relay-log.info` on the slave, can be retrieved without opening the files. Instead, using the `mysql` client, execute the SQL statement, SHOW SLAVE STATUS. On the next page is a sample of the results from this SQL statement. You can see how the values in the master information file match the values in the results.

Slave Status

When you look at the results on the next page, notice the labels for the additional SSL variables that were missing from at the end of the excerpt for `master.info` a couple of pages back. Again, that file contains lines for them, whether they are empty or populated. Also notice that as I mentioned before, for tighter security, the results here do not return the replication user account's password. After you've spent a little time looking over the results of SHOW SLAVE STATUS, we'll get back to the replication process.

Example 1.6: SHOW SLAVE STATUS Results

```
SHOW SLAVE STATUS \G

*********************** 1. row ***********************
              Slave_IO_State: Waiting for master
                              to send event
                 Master_Host: master_host
                 Master_User: replicant
                 Master_Port: 3306
               Connect_Retry: 60
             Master_Log_File: binary_log.000081
         Read_Master_Log_Pos: 9891236
              Relay_Log_File: relay.000005
               Relay_Log_Pos: 4179713
       Relay_Master_Log_File: binary_log.000081
            Slave_IO_Running: Yes
           Slave_SQL_Running: Yes
             Replicate_Do_DB:
         Replicate_Ignore_DB: mysql, test
          Replicate_Do_Table:
      Replicate_Ignore_Table:
     Replicate_Wild_Do_Table:
 Replicate_Wild_Ignore_Table:
                  Last_Errno: 0
                  Last_Error:
                Skip_Counter: 0
         Exec_Master_Log_Pos: 5272409
             Relay_Log_Space: 9353121
             Until_Condition: None
              Until_Log_File:
               Until_Log_Pos: 0
          Master_SSL_Allowed: No
```

Slave Status

```
              Master_SSL_CA_File:
              Master_SSL_CA_Path:
                 Master_SSL_Cert:
               Master_SSL_Cipher:
                  Master_SSL_Key:
           Seconds_Behind_Master: 9723
Master_SSL_Verify_Server_Cert: No
                   Last_IO_Errno: 0
                   Last_IO_Error:
                  Last_SQL_Errno: 0
                  Last_SQL_Error:
```

More Division of Labor in Slave

After noting the new position number and other information that may have changed, the slave uses the same I/O thread to resume waiting for more entries from the master. It will keep that channel open if it can. That thread focuses on just listening and taking data in, which, as mentioned above, just writes the data it receives to a relay log. It refuses to do anything else so as not to be distracted or bogged down. Therefore, a different thread is used to deal with implementing what was recorded in the slave's relay log.

When the slave server detects any change to its relay log, it uses an *SQL thread* to execute the new SQL statements recorded in the relay log in the slave's databases. After the new entry from the slave's relay log, the new relay log position identification number is recorded in its relay log information file (relay-log.info) through the slave's SQL thread. Below is the excerpt again from a relay log information file:

Example 1.7: Slave's relay-log.info File

```
/var/log/mysql/relay.000002
28839226
binary_log.000081
```

Now that you've looked over the results of the SQL statement, SHOW SLAVE STATUS on the previous page, let's compare and connect the field names to the contents of the relay-log.info file shown here.

The first line lists the file path and name of the current relay log file—this is the variable, Relay_Log_File in the results of the SHOW SLAVE STATUS statement. The second value is the SQL thread's position in the relay log file (the variable, Relay_Log_Pos). The third contains the name of the binary log file on the master from which the SQL thread successfully execute an event (Relay_Master_Log_File). The last value is the position in the master log file for the last executed event that was successful (Exec_Master_Log_Pos).

Incidentally, you may think it strange that all of these important details are kept in such miniscule text files. However, there's a reason and value in storing this data in text files. If the servers are shut down, or even powered off suddenly, the key bits of data will be preserved and replication can be resumed moderately easily. The master.info file belongs to the IO thread, which the relay-log.info file belongs to the SQL thread.

List of Slave Logs

When the slave is restarted, or its logs are flushed, it appends the name of the current relay log file to the end of the relay log index file (`relay-log.index`). An example of the contents of a relay log index file follows:

Example 1.8: Slave's relay-log.index File

```
/var/log/mysql/relay.000002
/var/log/mysql/relay.000003
/var/log/mysql/relay.000004
```

This is similar to the the `bin.index` file on the master, which keeps track of its logs. If an SQL thread is interrupted in processing the logs, it sorts through the logs and entries that it has in the same way as the master does on its end when the slave requests data. By this method, though, the slave doesn't have to ask the master again for data its already received—or risk duplicating data.

Again, this process of separating threads keeps the I/O thread free and dedicated to receiving changes from the master. It ensures that any delays in writing to the slave's databases on the SQL thread will not prevent or slow the receiving of data from the master. With this separate thread method, the slave server naturally has exclusive access to its relay log file at the file system level.

What will Stop a Slave

As an additional safeguard to ensure accuracy of data, the slave will compare entries in the relay log to the data in its databases. If the comparison reveals any inconsistency, the replication process is stopped and an error message is recorded in the slave's error log (`error.log`). It's up to you to notice that the slave has stopped replicating and to check its error log. The slave will not restart until it is told to do so—generally until its told. After you have resolved the discrepancy that the slave detected in the data, you can then instruct the slave to resume replication, as explained in Chapter 6, *Starting MySQL Replication*. If you don't resolve the discrepancy and try to restart replication of the slave, the slave will most likely stop again, fairly immediately.

The Slave's Error Log

To be able to resolve problems on a slave server, you'll have to read and understand its error log. Here is an example of what is recorded on a slave server in its error log when the results don't match:

Example 1.9: Slave's Error Log

```
100714 01:32:03  mysqld started
100714  1:32:05  InnoDB: Started
/usr/sbin/mysqld-max: ready for connections
100714  8:00:28  Slave SQL thread initialized,
   starting replication in log
   'server2-bin.035' at position 579285542,
   relay log './db1-relay-bin.001'
   position: 4
100714  8:00:29  Slave I/O thread: connected to master
   '...@66.216.68.90:3306', replication started in
   log 'server2-bin.035' at
   position 579285542 ERROR: 1146
   Table 'test.response' doesn't exist
100714  8:00:30  Slave: error 'Table 'test.response'
   doesn't exist' on query
'INSERT INTO response SET connect_time=0.073868989944458,
page_time=1.53695404529572, site_id='Apt'',
   error_code=1146
100714  8:00:30  Error running query,
```

The Slave's Error Log

```
    slave SQL thread aborted. Fix the
    problem, and restart the slave SQL thread with
    "SLAVE START". We stopped at
    log 'server2-bin.035' position 579285542
 100714  8:00:30  Slave SQL thread exiting,
    replication stopped in log
    'server2-bin.035' at position 579285542
 100714  8:00:54  Error reading packet from
    server:  (server_errno=1159)
 100714  8:00:54  Slave I/O thread killed while reading
 event
 100714  8:00:54  Slave I/O thread exiting, read up
    to log 'server2-bin.035', position 579993154
 100714  8:01:58  /usr/sbin/mysqld-max: Normal shutdown
 100714  8:01:58  InnoDB: Starting shutdown...
 100714  8:02:05  InnoDB: Shutdown completed
 100714  8:02:06  /usr/sbin/mysqld-max: Shutdown Complete
 100714 08:02:06  mysqld ended
```

In the first message that is bold-faced is an error message showing that the slave has realized that the relay log contains entries involving a table that does not exist on the slave. The second bold-faced bit of text gives a message informing the administrator of the decision and some instructions on how to proceed. Without the bold-facing I made here, a hefty error log file can be a confusing mess to sort through. That's why it's useful to know in advance what to look for before you have an emergency and are under pressure to solve the problem, quickly.

However, the error messages for which you will be searching will be near the end of the error log. As of version 5.1.20 of MySQL, you can find the error messages for the IO thread and for the SQL thread in the results of the SQL statement, SHOW SLAVE STATUS. These values are located at the end of its results table. Prior to MySQL 5.1.20, only the last error number and error message for the SQL thread was returned in the results. They're still there in the 15th and 16th fields (`Last_Errno` and `Last_Error`). I imagine that these fields will eventually be removed since they're respectively synonymous with `Last_SQL_Errno` and `Last_SQL_Error`.

Difficulty & Simplicity: A Summary

The MySQL Replication process may seem very involved and complicated at first, but all of it occurs quickly. As I mentioned before, it's typically not a significant drain on the master server's resources. Also, it's surprisingly easy to set up: it requires only a few lines of options in the configuration files on the master and slave servers. You will need to copy the databases on the master server to the slave to get the slave close to being current. Then it's merely a matter of starting the slave for it to begin replicating. The slave will rapidly update its data to record any changes since the initial back-up copied from the master was installed on the slave. Then replication will keep it current—theoretically. As an administrator you will have to monitor the replication process and resolve problems that arise occasionally.

Before concluding this chapter, let me adjust one of my statements above about the ease of replication: replication is deceptively simple. When it works, it's simple. Until it works, or if it stops working, the minimal requirements of replication make it difficult to determine why it doesn't work.

Difficulty & Simplicity: A Summary

Fortunately, the developers of MySQL have provided replication states, set messages about the state of replication on the slave. They also occasionally add to the list of possible replication states. This makes it easier to resolve problems, and to confirm your servers are in good states. The replication state is given in the results of SHOW SLAVE STATUS and SHOW PROCESSLIST. Replication states are discussed more throughout this book and in Appendix B. Now let's look at the steps for setting up replication in the next couple of chapters.

Chapter 2
Replication User Account

There are only a few steps to setting up MySQL Replication: set up a user account for replication activities, configure the master and slave servers for replication, then bulk copy the databases from the master to the slave server to prime the slave and then make sure that the slave has the name of the master's binary log and position at the time of the initial back-up. Then you just need to start the slave to get it caught up and to stay current.

Dedicated User Account

As mentioned above, the first step for setting up replication is to create user accounts dedicated to replication on both the master and the slave. For security reasons, it's best not to use an existing account. To set up the replication user account on the master, enter an SQL statement like the following on the master server, logged in as *root* or a user that has the GRANT OPTION privilege:

Example 2.1: Create Replication User

```
GRANT REPLICATION SLAVE, REPLICATION CLIENT ON *.*
TO 'replicant'@'slave_host' IDENTIFIED BY 'its_pwd';
```

Dedicated User Account

These two privileges are the only ones necessary for a user to replicate a server. The `REPLICATE SLAVE` privilege permits the user to connect to the master and to receive updates from the master's binary log.

The `REPLICATE CLIENT` privilege allows the user to execute the `SHOW MASTER STATUS` and the `SHOW SLAVE STATUS` statement. In this `GRANT` statement, the user account, *replicant* is granted only what is needed for replication. The user name can be almost anything. Both the user name and the host name are given within quotes. The host name can be one which is resolved through `/etc/hosts` (or the equivalent on your server's operating system), or it can be a domain name that is resolved through DNS. Or, you can instead give an IP address like so:

Example 2.2: Create User with IP Address

```
GRANT REPLICATION SLAVE, REPLICATION CLIENT ON *.*
TO 'replicant'@'12.127.17.72' IDENTIFIED BY 'its_pwd';
```

If you upgraded MySQL on your server and the `GRANT` statement shown above doesn't work, it may be because you were using a version in which these privileges didn't exist. Therefore, you will need to upgrade the server's `mysql` database—that's the core database of MySQL that contains user privileges and passwords, among other things. For information on fixing this problem, see Appendix C, the page on the utility, `mysql_fix_privilege_tables` or the page on the utility, `mysql_upgrade`, depending on the version of MySQL

Slave User Account

Once you've successfully executed the GRANT statement above on the master, enter it again on the slave server with the same user name and password, but with the master's host name or IP address instead of the slave's host information:

Example 2.3: Create Replication User on Slave

```
GRANT REPLICATION SLAVE, REPLICATION CLIENT ON *.*
TO 'replicant'@'master_host' IDENTIFIED BY 'its_pwd';
```

While it's not necessary that the user names be the same, there is a potential advantage of having the same user on both the master and the slave: If the master fails or will be down for a while, you could redirect users to the slave by changing your DNS information or by some other method. When the master is running again, you can then use replication to get the master up-to-date by temporarily making it a slave to the former slave server. Be aware that although this sounds sweet and would seem like a simple thing to do, it can be complicated. You should learn how to do it in advance, as well as experiment and practice with a couple of test servers before relying on it with production servers. You could lose data easily if you do it incorrectly. It could quickly be a mess. For more information on this topic, see Chapter 10, *Load Balancing*.

To see the results of the first GRANT statement for the master, enter the following on the master. The results follow.

Slave User Account

Example 2.4: SHOW GRANTS Statement

```
SHOW GRANTS FOR 'replicant'@'slave_host' \G

***** 1. row *****
Grants for replicant@slave_host:
GRANT REPLICATION SLAVE, REPLICATION CLIENT ON *.*
TO 'replicant'@'slave_host'
IDENTIFIED BY PASSWORD
'*60115BF697978733E110BA18B3BC31D181FFCG082'
```

Notice that the password shown here has been encrypted in the output by MySQL. If you don't receive results similar to those that are shown here, the GRANT statement entry failed. Check what you typed when you first granted the user privileges and when you executed this statement. If you typed incorrectly something like the user name and host, the simplest resolution might be to delete the user account and try again to create it. Deleting the user account won't be a problem since the account is not yet in use. To remove the account, enter something like the following on the server with the incorrect account:

Example 2.5: Delete User Account

```
REVOKE ALL ON *.*
FROM 'repliciant'@'slaves_host';
DROP USER 'repliciant'@'slaves_host';
```

Notice the keyword FROM in the REVOKE statement, instead of TO as in the GRANT statement from before. Notice that the user name and host name are spelled incorrectly here: supposedly as I might have mistyped

32, Part I: Understanding & Preparation

Slave User Account

them originally. You'll have to adjust this according to how you typed them. Now you only need to re-enter the `GRANT` statement as intended originally.

If everything was typed correctly and included in both statements, verify that you have version 4.0 of MySQL or higher, a version that supports these two new privileges. Execute `SELECT VERSION()` on each server to determine the versions they are using. It is also recommended that the master and slave servers are running the same versions of MySQL.

Slave User Account

Chapter 3
Configuring Servers

Although MySQL has the feature of replication built-in, to be able to start it you will need to configure the serves involved. One server should be designated as the master. This is generally the server which will contain the original data, the one to which users will add and change data. At least one other server will need to be designated as a slave. For the examples in this book, only one slave server is generally assumed. Additional servers are configured the same way, except that they will need to be given a different server identification number. As for physically connecting the master and slave servers to communicate with each other, they only need to be on the same network—this can even be across the internet. They don't need to be within proximity to each other.

Just to keep your bearing, let me outline briefly again the steps we're going through and where we are at this point: You will have to edit the option files on the master and the slaves. This is covered in this chapter. After this you will need to copy the data from the master to the slave to initialize it before starting the slave. This is covered in the subsequent chapters.

Configuring the Master

You will need to add some lines to the MySQL configuration file, the options file on the master. In the master's options file, you will only need to give it an identification number and activate binary logging. Even if you have a server which will not use replication, binary logging can be useful in resolving server problems or retrieving data lost since the last back-up.

Depending on the type of operating system, the configuration file will probably be called `my.cnf` or `my.ini`. On Unix types of systems, the configuration file is usually located in the `/etc` directory. On Windows systems, it's commonly placed in `c:\` or in `c:\Windows`. If the file doesn't exist on your system, you can create it. Using a plain text editor (e.g., `vi` or *Notepad.exe*), not an editor that won't add binary formatting (e.g., don't use *Word* or *WordPad*), add the following lines to the configuration file of the master under the `[mysqld]` group heading:

Example 3.1: Master's Options File

```
[mysqld]
server-id = 1
log-bin = /var/log/mysql/bin.log
...
```

The server identification number is an arbitrary number used to identify the master server in the binary log and in communications with slave servers. Almost any whole number from 1 to 4294967295 is fine. Don't use 0, as that causes problems. If you don't assign a server

Configuring the Master

number, the default server identification number of 1 will be used. For good form, though, assign a number in the options file. The number 1 for a server identification is alright for the master, but a different one should be assigned to each slave. To keep log entries straight and to avoid confusion in communications between servers, it is very important that each slave have a unique number.

In the configuration file excerpt just shown, the line containing the `log-bin` option instructs MySQL to perform binary logging to the path and file given. The actual file path and name is mostly up to you. Just be sure that the directory exists and that the file system user `mysql` is the owner, or at least has permission to write to the directory. By default, if a path is not given, the server's data directory is assumed as the path for log files. To leave the defaults in place, give `log-bin` without the equal-sign and without the path and file name. If you set the log file name to something else, keep the suffix `.log` as shown here. The suffix will be replaced automatically with an index number (e.g., .000001) as new log files are created, when the server is restarted or the logs are flushed. Incidentally, I add the ellipsis in the excerpt above and in other examples in this book to indicate that more may follow. You don't actually type the three dots.

The two options, `--server-id` and `--log-bin` are all that is required on the master. They can be put in the configuration file or given from the command-line when starting the `mysqld` daemon each time. On the command-line, add the required double dashes before

Chapter 3: Configuring Servers, 37

Configuring the Master

each option (i.e., `log-bin` becomes `--log-bin`) and omit any spaces around the equal-signs. For most options, the dashes between the text are switched to underscores when used in options files or as variables. It's recommended that you put the options in the options file, however, instead of entering them from the command-line: if an administrator restarts the server and forgets to include the `--log-bin`, binary logging will not be restarted and replication will fail. Recovering from that will require dumping all of the databases again and reinitializing data on the slave.

If you have InnoDB tables, you may want to add the following lines to the master's configuration file:

Example 3.2: Master's Options File - InnoDB

```
innodb_flush_log_at_trx_commit = 1
sync-binlog = 1
```

These resolve problems that can occur related to InnoDB and with transactions and binary logging.

Before moving on to configuring the slave, make sure that the master is binary logging. To do this, enter the following SQL statement on the master:

Example 3.3: SHOW log_bin Variable

```
SHOW VARIABLES LIKE 'log_bin';

+---------------+-------+
| Variable_name | Value |
+---------------+-------+
| log_bin       | ON    |
+---------------+-------+
```

Configuring the Master

If binary logging is running, the value ON, as it is here, should be returned.

The Slave Options File

On the slave server, you will need to add several options to the slave's configuration file, reflecting the greater complexity and number of threads on the slave. Put another way, more options indicates how replication is primarily the work of the slaves, not so much of the master.

You will have to provide the slave sever with an identification number, details on connecting to the master server, and more log options. To do this, add lines similar to the following to the slave's configuration file:

Example 3.4: Slave's Options File

```
[mysqld]
server-id = 2
report-host = slave_host

log-bin = /var/log/mysql/bin.log
log-bin-index = /var/log/mysql/log-bin.index
log-error = /var/log/mysql/error.log

relay-log = /var/log/mysql/relay.log
relay-log-info-file = /var/log/mysql/relay-log.info
relay-log-index = /var/log/mysql/relay-log.index

slave-load-tmpdir = /var/log/mysql/
skip-slave-start
...
```

At the top, you can see the server identification number is set to 2 here. Again, you can use any number, but don't use the same number used to identify the master

The Slave Options File

or another slave. The option `report-host` is used to register the slave so that it will appear in the results of SHOW SLAVE HOSTS when executed on the master. The next two stanzas above set the logs and related index files. If these files don't exist when the slave is started, it will automatically create them.

The second stanza starts binary logging as was done on the master server, but this time on the slave. This is the log that can be used to allow the master and the slave to reverse roles as mentioned earlier in this chapter. The binary log index file (`log-bin.index`) records the name of the current binary log file to use. The `log-error` option establishes an error log. Any problems with replication will be recorded in this log.

The next stanza defines the relay log (`relay-log`) that records each entry received from the master server's binary log, along with related files. The `relay-log-info-file` option names the path and name of the `relay-log.info` file. This file contains the file path and name of the current relay log file and the slave position in it. It also contains the file path and name of the last binary log on the master and the slave's position in it. The `relay-log-index` option points to the location and name of the relay log index file (`relay-log.index`), which contains a list of relay log files on the slave. Details of these files are described in Chapter 1, *MySQL Replication Process*.

The last stanza shows the `slave-load-tmpdir` option. This is necessary only if you expect to execute the LOAD DATA INFILE statement on the server. This SQL statement is used to import data in bulk from a text file

The Slave Options File

into the databases. The `slave-load-tmpdir` option specifies the temporary directory for those files. If you don't specify this option, the value of the `tmpdir` variable will be used. This option relates to replication because the slave will log `LOAD DATA INFILE` activities to the log files with the prefix `SQL_LOAD-` in this directory. For security, you may not want those logs to be placed in a directory such as `/tmp` since that directory is usually insecure.

The last option shown in the slave configuration file excerpt above, `skip-slave-start` prevents the slave from starting replication until you are ready. With this option, the slave will not start replicating until you execute the `START SLAVE` statement on the slave. The order and spacing of options as listed in the example above are a matter of personal style.

Master Connection

To set variables on the slave related to its connection with the master (e.g., the master's host address), it is recommended that you use the `CHANGE MASTER TO` statement on the slave. You could provide the values in the slave's configuration file. However, the slave will read the configuration file only the first time you start the slave for replication. Because the values are stored in the `master.info` file, MySQL relies on that file during subsequent start-ups and ignores these options in the main MySQL configuration file. The only time it adjusts the `master.info` file contents is when you tell it explicitly to change them with the `CHANGE MASTER TO` statement. You could edit the `master.info` file and

Master Connection

other replication information files directly, but the slave won't consult the file until you restart the slaves—besides, you might cause more problems in doing so. It's best to use the CHANGE MASTER TO statement to make changes, even when first setting up a slave. Here are examples of how to use this SQL statement:

Example 3.5: Setting Master Connection Info. on Slave

```
CHANGE MASTER TO MASTER_HOST = 'master_host';
CHANGE MASTER TO MASTER_PORT = 3306;
CHANGE MASTER TO MASTER_USER = 'replicant';
CHANGE MASTER TO MASTER_PASSWORD = 'its_pwd';
```

The set of SQL statements shown provide information about the master server. They are all executed on the slave, not the master, since it contains information on how the slave should connect to the master. The first SQL statement above gives the host name (or the IP address) of the master. The next one provides the port for the connection. Port 3306 is the default port for MySQL, but another could be used just for replication to improve performance or for security considerations. Of course, then you would have to establish more than one incidences of MySQL running on the master. The next two lines in the example above set the user name and password for logging into the master server. This is the user account that you set up just for replication, as described in Chapter 2, *Replication User Account*.

After the SQL statements above are executed, their values are stored in the master.info file discussed earlier and you shouldn't need to re-enter these

42, Part I: Understanding & Preparation

statements upon subsequent start-ups unless you want to use a different port or user, or maybe change the password for better security.

Ready for the Next Step

At this point, the servers should be configured properly. Next, you will need to get the slave primed. You'll do this by making a back-up of the master's databases and copying it to the slave. This is described in the following section. If the master and slave are new servers and the master has no data yet, you can skip the next two chapters and proceed to starting replication, covered in Chapter 6, *Starting MySQL Replication*.

Ready for the Next Step

Part II
Priming & Starting

If you're setting up replication with an existing server that already contains data, you will need to make an initial back-up of the databases and copy the back-up to the slave server. In the first chapter of this section, I explain the recommended method of doing this. In the second chapter, I provide some alternatives and comment on their limitations. The third chapter outlines how then to start replication.

To get a complete, static copy of your server's databases, you will either have to lock all of the tables in all of the databases which you make a back-up with mysqldump, or shut-down MySQL on the server while you copy the data directory of MySQL. The first choice may mean sluggish service on some systems as mysqldump makes a back-up. The second option is much quicker once you take MySQL off-line. However, for some administrators, being totally down, even for a minute may be worse than sluggish server for a few minutes. Either way, considering that once you set up replication you will probably have much more dependable service and good back-up protection, it may be worth inconveniencing users the one time.

The following chapter (Chapter 4) explains how to make a consistent back-up of the master's databases for replication using mysqldump. It also explains how to load that data onto the slave, properly. If you prefer not to use `mysqldump`, Chapter 5 explains how to shut down MySQL on the master and copy the data to the slave. It also explains slave settings that you'll have to set manually because of this method. The third chapter in this part, Chapter 6 goes through the steps for starting replication. In case replication doesn't start according to plan, the chapter gives advice and suggestions on troubleshooting the problem.

Chapter 4
Copying the Initial Data

At this point in setting up replication, you will need to make a back-up of the master's databases so that you can set up the initial data on the slave. The best back-up program for doing this is the utility `mysqldump` that comes with MySQL. It will create a text file containing SQL statements that can be executed on the slave to recreate the master's databases and their contents. This file is called a dump file. While `mysqldump` is generating the dump file, users will be able to access the data on the master, but not change it. This is known as read-only access. Don't worry: it won't take too long. Once the dump file is created, you can unlock the tables on the master, giving users read and write access again.

Once this is done, you can take your time and copy the dump file to your slave server. Then you'll load the dump file into MySQL on the slave. After that you can proceed to Chapter 6, *Starting MySQL Replication*, skipping Chapter 5, *Alternative Copying Methods*. You would read only that chapter if you don't want to use mysqldump to copy the master's data.

Dumping the Master Databases

When using `mysqldump`, for the purposes of setting up replication, there are a few options to use. Enter something like the following from the command-line on the master server:

Example 4.1: Export Master Databases

```
mysqldump --user=root --password=its_pwd \
        --extended-insert --all-databases \
        --ignore-table=mysql.users \
        --flush-logs --master-data \
> /home/russell/backup.sql
```

The back-slashes (i.e., \) at the end of each line indicate to the shell that more is to come on the next line and that the shell should wait before executing the command. Put another way, if you remove the back-slashes, you can enter of this on one long line. The greater-than sign at the beginning of the last line is to redirect the output of `mysqldump` to a file. The result of the above will be a text file (`backup.sql`) containing SQL statements to create all of the master's databases and tables and insert their data. Here is an explanation of some of the special options shown:

The `--extended-insert` option creates multiple-row, `INSERT` statements and thereby makes the resulting dump file smaller. It also allows the back-up to run faster. These are both desirable outcomes: the first for faster copying to the slave afterwards; the second for reducing the time which users are locked out of databases for writing.

Dumping the Master Databases

The `--ignore-table` option is used here so that the user names and passwords won't be copied. This is a good security precaution in general. However, that table probably won't be needed since the slave won't have the same users—especially if the slave will only be used for back-ups of the master. Unfortunately, there is no easy way to exclude the entire `mysql` database containing user information. You could list each table in that database to be excluded, but they have to be listed separately and that becomes cumbersome. The only table that contains passwords is the `users` table, so it may be the only one that matters. However, it depends on whether you set security on a database, table, or other basis, and therefore you may want to protect that user information. If you plan on using the slave for load balancing, besides using it as part of a back-up plan, you might want to include the `mysql.user` table. That way users on the master will be able to access data on the slave using the same user accounts and passwords.

The `--master-data` option shown in the example above locks all of the tables during the export to prevent data from being changed. It does allow users to continue reading the tables, though. This option also adds a few lines like the following to the end of the dump file:

Example 4.2: Dump File Excerpt with --master Option

```
-- --Position to start replication from --
CHANGE MASTER TO MASTER_LOG_FILE='bin.000846';
CHANGE MASTER TO MASTER_LOG_POS=427;
```

Dumping the Master Databases

When the dump file is executed on the slave server, these lines will record the name of the master's binary log file and the position in the log at the time of the back-up, while the tables were locked. This is important for a seamless transition. When replication is started, these lines will provide this information to the master so it will know the point in the master's binary log to begin sending entries to the slave. This is meant to ensure that any data that is changed while you set up the slave server isn't missed. This option requires the user to have RELOAD privilege on the master. A minor warning about these two statements: sometimes they aren't executed successfully when the dump file is loaded on the slave. You may have to enter them, manually. This is covered in the latter part of Chapter 6, *Starting Replication*.

The -flush-logs option will flush the logs on the master before the back-up begins. When this option is used in conjunction with --master-data, the logs on the master will be flushed only once when the tables are all locked for read only. Once the back-up finishes, the tables will be unlocked automatically. At this point, users will be able to change data again. For more information on these and other options are listed, see Appendix C, *MySQL Daemon & Utilities*.

Copy the Dump File to Slave

The next step at this point is to copy the back-up dump file to the slave and use it to load the databases and the data it contains on the slave. If you use FTP, make sure that you don't add any binary characters in the process

Copy the Dump File to Slave

with the FTP client. You might consider using the utility, `scp` to do a secure copy from the master to the slave. Here's an example of how you might use that command on a Unix type of file system:

Example 4.3: Copying from Master to Slave with scp

```
scp -v russell@master_host.com:/home/russell/backup.sql .
```

This will copy the dump file, `backup.sql` to the current directory—hence the single dot at the end. The `-v` option is to set the command to verbose so that the progress may be monitored. This may be useful with a large dump file.

Loading the Slave

After copying the dump file to the slave server, you'll need to load it into MySQL on the slave. To execute the dump file, MySQL will need to be running on the slave, but not replication. Meaning, don't execute the SQL statement, START SLAVE yet. To load the data, run the `mysql` client at a command-prompt on the slave like this:

Example 4.4: Load Back-up File with mysql Client

```
mysql --user=myback_admin \
      --password=its_pwd < /home/russell/backup.sql
```

This will execute all of the SQL statements contained in the dump file, creating a copy of the master's databases and data on the slave. It will run for quite a while, depending on the amount of data that's contained in the dump file. As a result, you may wonder if it's actually running or just locked up as it sits at the command-line

Chapter 4: Copying the Initial Data, 51

Loading the Slave

doing seemingly nothing. To reassure you that the SQL statements are being executed, you can add the option `--verbose` to the list of options in the command-line shown above. This option will display each SQL statement executed. Be careful, though. If left unattended, passers-by may observe sensitive data as its displayed on your monitor. Because of this, a better alternative is just to open a separate connection to MySQL with the `mysql` client and run a couple of `SELECT` statements to see for yourself that it's working. You can also execute the `SHOW PROCESSLIST` statement on the slave to verify the client is still running.

Skipping Ahead

Once the dump file is finished loading, the slave should be ready to start replication. Therefore, you can ship the next chapter and jump to Chapter 6, *Starting MySQL Replication*. The next chapter presents alternative, but not recommended methods of copying data from the master. If you've already done this with mysqldump as explained in this chapter, then you don't need the information in Chapter 5, *Alternative Copying Methods* and can skip it.

Chapter 5
Alternative Copying Methods

If you would prefer to use a different method than what was described in the previous chapter for making an initial copy of the master's databases to prepare a slave for replication, there are a couple of other ways of doing this. However, `mysqldump` is typically the easiest and simplest at this point. If you agree, skip this chapter. If not, this brief chapter presents some alternative methods to copy the the master's databases—and it disputes them.

A Simple SQL Statement

If you look through MySQL's documentation, you might spot the SQL statement, `LOAD DATA FROM MASTER` and think that it would be ideal for making an initial copy of a master's data on a slave server. However, it is actually not very feasible. First, it works only with MyISAM tables. Tables using other storage engines will not be copied. That may be fine for some databases which only use the MyISAM storage engine. Second, because this SQL statement causes a global read lock to be invoked on the master server while it's making a back-up, it

A Simple SQL Statement

prevents the master from serving users for some time. So, copying data across a network or the internet could mean that master will be down for a very long time.

Unlike the method described in the previous chapter on `mysqldump`, this SQL statement doesn't lock users out, and then unlock the server, and then copy the data to the slave, and then load the data on the slave. It does it all in one very slow step with users blocked the whole time. During that slow step, if a network problem occurs or something else interrupts the process, it will stop and you will have to start the SQL statement again.

Basically, the `LOAD DATA FROM MASTER` statement was a good idea on the part of the developers. However, it turned out to be not very useful or practical in almost all situations. As a result, it has been deprecated and will be removed from future releases of MySQL. So, don't use it.

Raw Copying of Data

Another alternative to using `mysqldump` is to copy the raw files containing the schemata and data from the command-line. You won't be able to use this method of copying the master's data directory if you don't have administrative access to the filesystems or if you don't have permissions to the data directories. Also, be aware that you will run into a complication with this method if you have InnoDB tables in your databases. Their data is not stored in the default data directory.

Raw Copying of Data

For these reasons `mysqldump` remains the recommended method for copying initially the master's data in preparation for setting up a slave server for replication. However, if you still prefer this method and have the necessary permissions, I explain this method in the rest of this chapter.

Locking Tables and Taking Notes

As mentioned when using `mysqldump`, binary logging will need to be running (see Chapter 3, *Configuring Servers*). If you don't want to shut down the master server completely while making a copy of its data, you can leave it running but prevent changes to its data by putting a read-only lock on the tables. A read-only lock will allow users to be able to retrieve data from MySQL, but not write data. You would do this by entering the following SQL statement on the master:

Example 5.1: Locking Tables

```
FLUSH TABLES WITH READ LOCK;
Query OK, 0 rows affected (0.00 sec)
```

Since this statement will commit any transactions that may be occurring on the server, it may take a moment to complete the lock. So be careful and make sure the lock is actually in place before you continue—wait for the *Query OK* message, as shown above, after executing the statement. There is no way to know for sure that all of the tables are locked when you enter the statement. However, if the lock was not successful, an error will be

Locking Tables and Taking Notes

returned. If it was successful, until you unlock it or close your session by exiting the `mysql` client, the tables will stay locked.

Before starting to copy the data, you should make a note of the name of master's binary log file, where the master is in that binary log.

Example 5.2: Master Status
```
SHOW MASTER STATUS \G

*********** 1. row ************
            File: binary_log.000081
        Position: 100172500
    Binlog_Do_DB:
Binlog_Ignore_DB:
```

As you can see from the results here, this SQL statement will provide you with the name of the current binary log file and the master's current position in the log. Write down or copy this information. You will need this to start replication on the slave, to get the changes made to the master's data after the back-up is made.

Now copy the master's data directory to an alternative directory. If you don't know the file path of your data directory, execute the following SQL statement on the master server:

Example 5.3: Master's Data Directory Variable
```
SHOW VARIABLES LIKE 'datadir';
```

This will return the absolute path of where data is contained on the server. You will need to copy everything in this directory and all sub-directories of it.

Once you've finished copying the data directory, execute the UNLOCK TABLES statement on the master using the mysql client. After that, the server will respond to users as usual.

Copy the Master's Data

The next task is to transfer the copy you made of the master's data directory to the slave server. If you use an FTP client to transfer the data to the slave, make sure the FTP client doesn't add binary codes to the file. This will cause problems with MySQL. A better alternative is the utility, scp for making secure copies. Below is an example of how you might use this utility:

Example 5.4: scp Copying Data from Master to Slave

```
scp -v myadmin@master_host:/data/backup/ /data/mysqlprep/
```

This will copy the directory /data/backup/ and all of its sub-directories on the master to the directory /data/mysqlprep/ on the slave. Be sure that both directories are secure. Don't copy the files directly to the data directory.

Once you have copied the files to the slave, determine the location of the MySQL data directory on the slave. You can do this by executing the SHOW VARIABLE statement as shown above, but on the slave. Then shutdown MySQL on the slave. You can do that usually by entering the following from the command-line:

Example 5.5: Shutting Down MySQL

```
mysqladmin shutdown
```

Copy the Master's Data

When this is done, copy the files from the master to the data directory, being careful not to overwrite the sub-directory for the `mysql` database. Keep the one installed on the slave. So you'll just copy the sub-directories for your databases.

After the copying is finished, be sure to change the ownership of all of the files and sub-directories to the file system user, `mysql`. In Linux, this is done by entering the following statement as *root*:

Example 5.6: Change Ownership of Data Directory

```
chown -R mysql:mysql /path_to_data
```

If your server is using a different operating system, you'll have to figure out how to do the same thing on it.

You're now ready to start MySQL on the slave. Just don't start replication yet. So start MySQL however you might normally start it. On a Linux system you might start it like this:

Example 5.7: Starting MySQL at command-line in Linux

```
/etc/rc.d/init.d/mysql start
```

Each system seems to have its own method for starting MySQL. So, I'll leave it you to determine how to do this on your system.

Setting Master Position

Once MySQL is running on the slave, log into MySQL with the `mysql` client and check the data. Try executing the SHOW DATABASES, statement and similar statements to ensure the masters data has been loaded on the slave.

If the copy of the data was successful, you will need to inform the slave of the master's binary log information. You can do this by executing the CHANGE MASTER TO statement like this:

Example 5.8: Setting Master Position

```
CHANGE MASTER TO MASTER_BINARY_LOG=binary_log.000081;
CHANGE MASTER TO MASTER_LOG_POS=100172500;
```

The details for these entries were taken from the results you wrote down from when you executed SHOW MASTER STATUS. If you didn't do that when you had a lock on the tables and copied the master's data directory, it's too late now. You'll have to start over, locking, and copying the master's data again.

After you successfully execute the CHANGE MASTER TO statements, your slave is ready to connect to the master and to start replication. When it does, the slave will get any changes that occurred since you copied the data across. This is covered in the next chapter.

Setting Master Position

Chapter 6
Starting MySQL Replication

After you create the replication user accounts, configured properly the master and slave servers, and loaded the backed-up databases onto the slave server, you're ready to begin replication. Remember, on the master side, if it's making binary logs, it's already prepared. All the master needs is to know that another server wants to have a replication relationship with it. So, execute the following SQL statement on the slave while logged in as *root* or a user with SUPER privileges:

Example 6.1: Starting Replication

```
START SLAVE;
```

After this statement is executed, the slave should connect to the master and get the changes it missed since the initial back-up was made. Remember, the slave knows the point in the master's binary log from which it needs to start replicating because you ran mysqldump with the --master-data option. When you loaded the data from the dump file, it should have informed the slave of the binary log file name and position. If you didn't use mysqldump, but copied the data directory as described in the previous chapter, you should have done this manually—also explained in the same chapter. So, once you execute `START SLAVE`, the slave should stay current by continuously interacting with the master.

If everything is configured correctly on the slave, it will most likely start without a problem and return no message when `START SLAVE` is executed. However, when the slave tries to connect to the master, the connection may fail. Or when the SQL thread begins processing entries received from the master, it may fail. For whatever reason, if a slave fails after it's started, the `mysql` client or whatever client you used to try to start the slave process will not be informed of the failure. There won't be an error message or confirmation of any kind. Nor will it be informed of the subsequent termination of the slave threads. For that information, you will have to read the slave's error logs.

To confirm a slave is running, you can execute the following SQL statement from the slave:

Example 6.2: Slave Status

```
SHOW SLAVE STATUS \G
```

Example 1.6 in Chapter 1 shows an example of how the results may look. On your slave server, look for the variables, `Slave_IO_Running` and `Slave_SQL_Running` (the eleventh and twelfth variables). They should both say, `Yes`. If one of them has a value of `No`, check the value of the first variable, `Slave_IO_State` to see what is the replication state of the slave. In Appendix B, *MySQL Replication States*, the various states are described.

You should also look at the values for the last four variables of the results of SHOW MASTER STATUS, the ones regarding error numbers and messages for the IO and SQL threads. These will get you started resolving any problems. However, there are a few common problems that administrators have when first setting up and starting MySQL Replication. I cover them in the remaining pages of this chapter.

If your slave is running correctly and without any error messages, you're finished with this chapter. When you're ready to begin reaping the benefits of replication (e.g., clean and simple back-ups, load balancing), then you can begin reading Part III, *Administration*. When you encounter snags with MySQL Replication, remember that you can find information on replication states in Appendix B. This will help you sort through replication problems. For now, congratulations on setting up replication successfully.

Network and User Problems

If the slave didn't start, you probably have one or more basic problems. First you should make sure that you have a network connection from the slave server to the master with the replication user. You can check this by simply logging into the master, but remotely from the slave. On the slave enter something like this from the command-line:

Example 6.3: Remote Login with Replication User

```
mysql --host=master_host --user=replicant \
      --password=its_pwd
```

Network and User Problems

If all is set correctly, you should be able to log in. You won't have access to many of the databases since the user account has very limited privileges. However, if this fails—unless you typed incorrectly the options or login information—then you have either a network problem or you don't have your replication user set up correctly. To verify it's not a network problem, try the usual methods of checking (e.g., `ping` the master). Then try logging in with another MySQL user if you already have one that works from the slave to the master—it's unlikely you do, though.

If the network connection is fine, verify the user account by entering this SQL statement from the master:

Example 6.4: Checking Replication User Privileges

```
SHOW GRANTS FOR 'replicant'@'slave_host' \G

*******1. row *****
Grants for replicant@slave_svr:
   GRANT REPLICATION SLAVE, REPLICATION CLIENT
   ON *.* TO 'replicant'@'slave_host'
   IDENTIFIED BY PASSWORD '57fa123ada3c5c9k34'
```

Your results should read like the results above. The replicant user account should have `REPLICATION SLAVE` and `REPLICATION CLIENT` privileges. If you used a host name instead of an IP address for the host as I did here, make sure that the host name can be resolved back to your slave's IP address: check the slave's DNS information or maybe `/etc/hosts` on Unix type of systems.

Network and User Problems

If you receive Error 1141, saying that *"There is no such grant defined for user 'replciant' on host 'slave_host'"*, you either typed the users name or host wrong when you first set up the user, or your attempt to set up the user failed. If you remember setting up the user successfully, check to see if you made a typing error by entering the following SQL statement on the master:

Example 6.5: Listing Users on Master

```
SELECT User, Host
FROM mysql.user
ORDER BY User;

+------------------+---------------+
| User             | Host          |
+------------------+---------------+
| admin_backup     | localhost     |
| replciant        | slaves_hosts  |
| root             | localhost     |
| russell          | home_server   |
+------------------+---------------+
```

This will list all of the user accounts on the master. Look through the results for the replication user account. If you see the user account, but with either the user or host information incorrect, you should delete the user account and then create it again. In the results above you can see the user name and host are incorrect. To fix this, you would enter the following:

Example 6.6: Deleting and Re-Creating Replication User

```
REVOKE ALL ON *.* FROM 'replciant'@'slaves_hosts';

DROP USER 'replciant'@'slaves_hosts';

GRANT REPLICATION SLAVE, REPLICATION CLIENT
ON *.* TO 'replicant'@'slave_host'
IDENTIFIED BY 'its_pwd';
```

Network and User Problems

After doing all of this, try again to log remotely into the master from the slave. If it now works, try again to start the slave with `START SLAVE` and check again the results of `SHOW SLAVE STATUS` on the slave to see if replication is running.

Master Info Problems

If you're able to log remotely into the master from the slave using the replication user account, but still can't start the slave replicating, the master connection information may be incorrect on the slave. Look at the results of `SHOW SLAVE STATUS` again and see if the variables `Master_Host`, `Master_User`, and `Master_Port` are correct. See if they're the same host and user name that you used to connect manually to the master. Make sure the port number is correct. It should be 3306, unless you set this specifically to use a different port. Next check that the slave has the correct password for the replication user. To do this, you need to check the `master.info` file, usually located in the data directory for MySQL. To determine that directory, enter this SQL statement on the slave:

Example 6.7: Determining the Data Directory

```
SHOW VARIABLES LIKE 'datadir';

+---------------+--------------+
| Variable_name | Value        |
+---------------+--------------+
| datadir       | /data/mysql/ |
+---------------+--------------+
```

66, Part II: Priming & Starting

Master Info Problems

Take the file path it returns to be able to open the `master.info` file. Assuming it's in that directory, enter something like the following on a Unix type of system:

Example 6.8: Displaying the `master.info` File Contents

```
cat /data/mysql/master.info
```

In the master.info file, wedges between the replication user and the port number, there should be the replication user's password in plain text. Probably the sixth line—that may change in future versions of MySQL. If any of these bits of data are incorrect or missing, use the CHANGE MASTER TO statement to add or change them. Don't manually change them in the `master.info` file. This file and all are explained in Chapter 3, *Configuring Servers*. Here are the SQL statements you would enter on the slave for these four settings:

Example 6.9: Setting Master Connection Info. on Slave

```
CHANGE MASTER TO MASTER_HOST = 'master_host';
CHANGE MASTER TO MASTER_USER = 'replicant';
CHANGE MASTER TO MASTER_PASSWORD = 'its_pwd';
CHANGE MASTER TO MASTER_PORT = 3306;
```

After this is done, check the `master.info` file again for good measure and so that you can see the effect of what you just did. It helps to solidify the learning process. Assuming that went through alright, try starting the slave again and verify it's running.

Now What's Wrong?

If replication still isn't running after you have verified all of the previous common problems, you seem to have a more than basic problem getting replication going. You'll have to check the slave's error log for `mysqld`. Enter the following on the slave with the `mysql` client:

Example 6.10: Locating the Slave's Error Log

```
SHOW VARIABLES LIKE 'log_error';
+---------------+----------------------+
| Variable_name | Value                |
+---------------+----------------------+
| log_error     | /var/log/mysqld.log  |
+---------------+----------------------+
```

This should give you the absolute path and file name for the error log of `mysqld`. If it returns nothing, you may have to add the `--log-error` option to the slave's options file (i.e., `my.cnf` or `my.ini`) and restart MySQL on the slave.

Once you have the file path and name of the error log, view the tail end of the error log to see what is happening when you try to start the slave. On a Unix type of system, you can enter something like the following from the command-line on the slave:

Example 6.11: Monitoring the Slave's Error Log

```
tail -f /var/log/mysqld.log
```

This will start by showing you the last ten lines of the `mysqld.log` file. Now open another terminal window and log into MySQL and execute the `START SLAVE` statement yet again. Then look back at the `mysqld` log to read the new messages that are logged related to

Now What's Wrong?

your attempt to start replication. This will tell you what is bothering it when it tries to start replication. From there you'll have to try to resolve the problem based on what it tells you.

If you can't figure it out for yourself, you can try to get help from the MySQL community by posting a message on the MySQL forum for replication (*http://forums.mysql.com/list.php?26*). If you do post a message, you should copy the error messages from `msyqld.log` into your post. You should also explain in your post that you verified that you have the correct user account information on the slave for connecting to the master. The community is pretty quick in responding and is often helpful.

Summary

Once the slave is running without errors, you're finished with this part of the book. Since MySQL, when starting replication successfully, provides no fanfare, let me say in its stead, congratulations. Take a break and feel proud of yourself. When you're ready, you can move on to the next part of this book to claim some of t he benefits of replication. It will explain hot to set up back-ups on the slave, as well as provide tips on restoring a back-up. It will also give you suggestions on monitoring MySQL Replication, and introduce you to load balancing —the coolest part of using replication.

Summary

Part III
Replication Administration

Generally, there are two primary reasons for setting up replication with MySQL. The first reason is to be able to make back-ups of MySQL data easier, to make them consistent and without interruption of service to users. The second reason for struggling to set up replication is to improve performance—that is to say, for load balancing of user traffic in MySQL. This part covers these two topics in separate chapters: backing up the slave and load balancing.

As an administrator, in addition to being able to back-up the slave's databases, you will have to restore occasionally data from back-ups. Otherwise, what's the point of making back-ups? While this is not directly part of replication, since a primary reason for replication is to make back-ups, a chapter on restoring data from a back-up is included in this part of the book.

Finally, to ensure proper back-ups, one has to ensure that replication is running as it should. For this, I have included a chapter on checking automatically that slave is running and checking its replication states.

Chapter 7
Backups with Replication

With replication running, it's an easy task to make a back-up of the data. You just need to stop temporarily the slave server from replicating and then make the back-up on the slave. You can use any back-up utility or method you prefer. However, I recommend using mysqldump. It's the simplest method and its back-up files are the most portable. I explain how to make a back-up using this utility. If you want to use another back-up utility, just substitute references to mysqldump in my examples with your chosen utility.

Stopping Replication

Before beginning a back-up on the slave, you should stop replication on the slave. To do this, enter the following SQL statement while logged onto the slave server as *root* or any user with SUPER privileges:

Example 7.1: Stopping Replication on a Slave

```
STOP SLAVE;
```

Stopping Replication

This will stop replication only for the slave on which you execute it. You don't have to worry about the slave missing data, though, while it's not replicating. The slave server knows the point where it stopped replicating in the binary log of the master server and has recorded that information in its `master.info` file. Nor do you have to inform the master that the slave will be down for a while. It's used to being ignored by slaves. So you can take your time making a back-up of the replicated databases on the slave server.

The only complication you may have is if the slave also assists in handling user requests for load balancing. In which case, `STOP SLAVE` throws the burden back on the master or on other slaves for handling user traffic. If you set up load balancing, you have to prepare for slaves to be stopped when you plan out your load balancing strategy.

Still, for making back-ups on slaves in which users access, you just need to lock the tables for read only. This way users won't change the data on the slave during the back-up. For slaves that are designated only in a load balancing plan for user read queries and no user writes, making a back-up will have little effect on them.

To make a back-up on the slave with `mysqldump`, enter something like the following at the command-line on the slave server:

Example 7.2: Making a Back-up on a Slave

```
mysqldump --user=myback_admin --password=its_pwd \
        --flush-logs --master-data --all-databases \
    > /back-ups/mysql/backup.sql
```

Stopping Replication

As mentioned in earlier chapters, this will create a dump file which will contain all of the SQL statements necessary to reconstruct all of the databases on the server along with their data. You may notice that I have included the option, `--flush-logs` and `--master-data`. This `--flush-logs` option will put a read-only lock on all tables and all databases for the duration of the back-up. This way the data will be consistent between tables and databases. This duration lock only occurs when this option is used with the `--master-data` option. That option includes the `CHANGE MASTER TO` statements related to the master's binary log and the slave's position in that log at the time of the back-up. While it might seem unnecessary to include these statements, if you ever need to use the back-up to restore the slave, you will need to know where the slave left off in replication at the time of the back-up. This will allow you to do a full restore or overwrite of the slave's databases. Then the master, through replication can help the slave with the data it's missing since the back-up. If you use the back-up to restore the master, you can just delete the `CHANGE MASTER TO` statements from the master if you are concerned about them causing problems. They won't. For more information on `mysqldump` and its options, see Appendix C of this book.

Back to Replicating

When the back-up is finished, you will need to restart replication on the slave. Enter the following SQL statement as *root* or a user account with SUPER privileges on the slave server to restart replication:

Example 7.3: Starting Replication

START SLAVE;

After entering this SQL statement, there should be a flurry of activity on the slave as it executes the SQL statements that occurred while the slave wasn't replicating. In a very short period of time, though, it should be current again. You can enter the SQL statement SHOW SLAVE STATUS on the slave to check its status. See Example 1.6 in Chapter 1 or Appendix A, *Statements and Functions* for examples of the results of this statement, as well as explanations of it. However, it's better if you run it on your server at this point.

When you do execute SHOW SLAVE STATUS, in particular, look for the values for Slave_IO_Running and Slave_SQL_Running. They each should say *Yes* if the slave is connected to the master—even if it's waiting for updates. On older versions of MySQL, Slave_SQL_Running would have a value of *No* when it wasn't processing any data changes.

Conversely, you can run the SQL statement, SHOW PROCESSLIST on the master. Below are sample results from that statement, but only for the row related to a replication slave:

Example 7.4: `SHOW PROCESSLIST` *Results*

```
SHOW PROCESSLIST \G

...
*********************** 8. row ***********************
     Id: 1908
   User: home_replicant
   Host: home_svr:44314
     db: NULL
Command: Binlog Dump
   Time: 36843
  State: Has sent all binlog to slave;
         waiting for binlog to be updated
   Info: NULL
```

In this example, the State field shows that the master has given all updates from the binary log to the slave and the two of them are waiting for changes to be made by users. This state and other replication states are described in Appendix B of this book.

Automating Back-ups

In order for back-ups to be most effective, they need to be performed regularly. To ensure this, you should create a script or program to run `mysqldump`, automatically. To assist you in writing such a program, on the next page I have provided a basic program written in Perl which will do this task daily.

Code Example 7.1: Daily Back-up

```perl
#!/usr/bin/perl -w

# Set Variables for Backup File Name & Path
use POSIX 'strftime';
my $date = strftime("%Y%m%d", localtime(time));
my $dir = '/data/backups';
```

Code Example 7.1: Daily Back-up

```perl
# Concat together Backup File Name
my $backup_file = 'mysql_backup_' . $date . '.sql';

# MySQL Connection Parameters
my $user = 'myback_admin';
my $pwd = 'its_pwd';
my $host = 'localhost';
my $db = 'db1';

# Connect to MySQL & Stop Replication
my $dbh = DBI->connect(qq|DBI:mysql:$db;
        host=$host;user=$user;password=$pwd|,
        undef, undef, {RaiseError=>1})
     || die 'Could not connect to MySQL: '
        . DBI->errstr;
$dbh->do('STOP SLAVE', undef, undef);

# Put together mysqldump with options and Execute
my $dump_command = "mysqldump -user=$user "
                 . "--password=$pwd "
                 . "--all-databases "
                 . " > $dir$backup_file";
system($dump_command);

# Check if Successful and Inform User
if ($? == -1) { print "Successful. \n" }
else { print "Unable to back-up databases. \n" }

# Restart Replication on Slave
$dbh->do('START SLAVE', undef, undef);
$dbh->disconnect();

exit;
```

This program will create an SQL dump file which will be named `mysql_backup_yyyymmdd.sql`, with the date part modified based on the date in which it is run. To get the date, this program uses the *POSIX* Perl module and the `strftime( )` function from it to format the date. It stores the date in a variable to be able to put together the back-up file name later. In the second stanza of this Perl program, the MySQL related variables

Code Example 7.1: Daily Back-up

are set up which will be used a few times. In the third stanza, the program connects to MySQL and stops the slave. The next couple of stanzas put together the back-up file name and the `mysqldump` command with the needed options to dump all of the databases. The Perl function, `system( )` is used to execute the variable containing the `mysqldump` line with options at the file system level. The next stanza checks what is returned by the `system( )` function and informs the user. The last stanza of this program restarts the slave and disconnects from MySQL. The program then exits.

This Perl program isn't as thorough as it could be. There is very little error checking or reporting. Still, it gives you an idea of what you can do to automate back-ups on a slave server.

As an alternative to Perl, you can create a shell script that you could execute on a Unix type of system. Here's an example of such a script:

Code Example 7.2: Daily Back-up

```
#!/bin/sh

date = `date +%Y%m%d`

mysqladmin -user=bkadmn --password=its_pwd stop-slave

mysqldump --user=bkadmn --password=its_pwd \
          --opt --all-databases \
          > /data/backups/mysql_backup_${date}.sql

mysqladmin --user=bkadmn --password=its_pwd start-slave
```

Code Example 7.2: Daily Back-up

In this script, the utility, `mysqladmin` is used to stop replication on the slave at the beginning and to start it again at the end. For naming the back-up files, the system function `date` is used to record the date in a variable which is aptly named *date*. The system function `date` also puts it into the same format as used in the Perl program. The result will be to generate a file named, `mysql_backup_`*yyyymmdd*`.sql`, or rather, something like `mysql_backup_20100115.sql`. Notice that the `date` function and the formatting codes are enclosed within back-ticks, not single-quotes.

Again, like the Perl program, this is a simple script. You probably should write one more elaborate to include error checking. You may also want to compress the dump files to save space. The primary difference between this shell script and the Perl program is that this one is shell based and it uses file system functions and command-line utilities.

Once you have written your own back-up script, test it manually a few times. When you're satisfied that it's functioning dependably, then add it to a scheduler program like `crontab` to run during slow traffic times. Actually, since its for a replication server, it probably doesn't matter when you run the back-up script. You could even make back-ups several times a day if you want, without worrying about draining MySQL resources.

Tweaking a Slave Start

By default, the START SLAVE statement starts both the I/O thread and the SQL thread. However, if you don't want to start both slave threads, you can specify which one to start when using the START SLAVE statement. You can also specify a particular master binary log file and the position in the log in which to *stop* replicating. You shouldn't need to make these distinctions when first starting a slave, though. Still, these extra options for START SLAVE are useful when debugging a problem with a slave log, and especially when attempting to restore data to a particular position in the log because a user entered an erroneous statement or if you want to revert to an earlier point in the database. Here's an example of these possibilities:

Example 6.12: Tweaking the Start of the Slave

```
START SLAVE SQL_THREAD
UNTIL MASTER_LOG_FILE = 'relay.0000052',
MASTER_LOG_POS = 254;
```

You can also control the processing of the slave's relay log file with the same syntax shown, but using the RELAY_LOG_FILE and the RELAY_LOG_POS parameters instead. You cannot specify a master log position and a relay log position in the same statement, though.

The UNTIL clause of this SQL statement will be ignored if the SQL thread is already running. It will also be ignored if a slave which is already running replication is shut down and restarted, or if the STOP SLAVE statement is executed followed by a START SLAVE statement without the UNTIL clause. Therefore, to use these options for

Tweaking a Slave Start

fine-grained control, restart MySQL on the slave server with the `--skip-slave-start` option in the configuration file so that both threads won't be restarted inadvertently.

Chapter 8
Restoring a Back-up

If you lose your data in MySQL, but have been using regularly `mysqldump` to make back-ups of your data, you can use the dump files to restore your data: this is the point of the back-ups, after all. To restore a `mysqldump` file, it's just a matter of having the `mysql` client execute all of the SQL statements that the file contains. This was discussed in Chapter 4 on using `mysqldump` to prime a slave server with initial data copied from the master. However, since replication is often used as a component of making consistent back-ups, I've included more details on the concept of restoring data from `mysqldump`, not directly related to replication.

Simple, Blunt Restore

There are some factors to consider before restoring MySQL data from a dump file. One simple and perhaps clumsy method to restore from a dump file is to enter something like the following:

Example 8.1: Executing a Dump File

```
mysql --user=admin_restore --password \
   < /data/backups/mysql_backup_20100115.sql
```

Simple, Blunt Restore

Again, this doesn't use `mysqldump`. The `mysqldump` utility is only for making back-up copies, not for restoring databases. Instead, we're using the `mysql` client which will read the dump file's contents in order to batch execute the SQL statements that it contains.

Notice in the example above that the redirect for standard output (`stdout`) is not used here, but instead the redirect for the standard input (`stdin`); the less-than sign is used since the dump file is an input source. Notice also that in this example a database isn't specified. That's given within the dump file. If you're restoring a master, you may want to stop access to the master by users before performing a restore, and then start it again when done. This includes stopping replication on slaves with the `STOP SLAVE` statement. Of course, while the master is down you can redirect users to the slave—at least for reading data. Writing data might be more complicated than you like. Redirecting read requests to a slave will at least take the pressure off of you while you restore the data. So it's worth looking into and practicing before a crisis.

You can use a variety of methods to redirect users to a slave (e.g., change your DNS or the server's virtual IP address, temporarily). This topic is covered in Chapter 10, *Load Balancing*.

Restoring from a Slave

When restoring a master server from a dump file made by `mysqldump`, you may only be able to restore the data up until the last back-up. If the master crashed without

Restoring from a Slave

disturbing the databases on the slave, then you could make a back-up of the slave's databases with `mysqldump` and restore the master from it. So that the slave won't log any of the events generated on the master while it's being restored, not only should you stop the slave from replicating, but you might want to disable the master from logging the activities. To do this latter piece and to restore the back-up, you would enter the following from the command-line on the master:

Example 8.2: Executing a Dump File

```
cd /data/backups/

scp -v russell@slave_host:/data/backups/
mysql_backup_20100301.sql .

echo 'SET SQL_LOG_BIN = 0;' |
   cat - mysql_backup_20100301.sql \
   >mysql_backup_20100301.sql.tmp

mysql --user=admin_restore --password \
   < /data/backups/mysql_backup_20100301.sql.tmp
```

In this example, a dump file was made on the slave. It's called, `mysql_backup_20100301.sql`. It's copied to the master first using the `scp` utility—it's entered in one long line that is wrapping here. Using the shell command, echo, we are appending a SET statement to the beginning of the dump file. You could also add this SQL statement to the dump file with a simple text editor. The purpose of the statement is to stop binary logging for the session. This can only be done on a session basis and not globally—at least not easily. Disabling binary logging will prevent the slaves which have correct data from coping the restore, thus duplicating or at least draining system resources significantly. The echo basically creates a new dump file with the SQL statement at the beginning. So on the last line above, we restore that file to the server. Be sure to remove both back-up files when you're finished. You don't have to worry about enabling binary logging when the restore is finished since it only affects the restore session of the `mysql` client and the disable ends automatically when the session ends.

One Database, One Table Only

The problem with restoring from a dump file is that you may end up overwriting tables or databases that you wish you hadn't. For instance, your dump file might be a few days old and only one table may have been lost. If you restore all databases or all tables in a database, you would be restoring the data back to it's state at the time of the back-up, a few days before. This could be quite a disaster. Making separate dumps by database and tables instead of all databases in one dump file can be handy. However, that could be cumbersome on some servers.

A simple and easy method of limiting a restoration would be to create temporarily a user who will have only privileges for the table you want to restore. You would enter GRANT statements like the following ones on the master—or whichever server to which you're restoring data:

One Database, One Table Only

Example 8.3: Creating a Limited Restoration User Account

```
GRANT SELECT
ON db1.* TO 'restore_temp'@'localhost'
IDENTIFIED BY 'its_pwd';

GRANT ALL ON db1.table1
TO 'restore_temp'@'localhost';
```

These two SQL statements allow the temporary user to have the needed SELECT privileges on all tables of the database, *db1* and ALL privileges for the table, *table1*, which includes the privileges necessary to overwrite data for *table1*. Now when you restore the dump file containing all of the databases, only *table1* will be replaced with the back-up copy—for the other tables in *db1*, permission will be denied when you try to overwrite them. The same will happen for other databases. Of course, MySQL will generate errors. To overlook the errors and to proceed with restoring data for tables the user has permission to overwrite (i.e., just *table1*), the --force option is used. Below is what you would enter at the command-line for this situation:

Example 8.4: Restoring with Limited User Account

```
mysql --user restore_temp --password --force \
    < /data/backups/mysql_backup_20100115.sql
```

Again, this will generate multiple errors for tables and databases to which the user *restore_temp* has no privileges, but they will be ignored and not displayed. Instead, only the table, *table1* will be restored. You may want to disable binary logging as shown in the Example 8.2, by adding a line at the top of the dump file to set the SQL_LOG_BIN variable to 0.

Chapter 8: Restoring a Back-up, 87

One Database, One Table Only

The alternative to this trick of restoring only one table based on user privileges is to edit the dump file and delete the other tables or extract the SQL statements related to `table1` and copy them into a text file and then feed the file to the `mysql` client the same as above. While this approach may seem easier than the previous one, it can be cumbersome and not simpler if you need to restore multiple tables in different databases. Giving a temporary user privileges to all tables to be restored can prove simpler, especially in such a situation.

Chapter 9
Monitoring Replication

Although replication is an excellent feature of MySQL, things can happen which will cause replication to stop. For instance, some internet service providers will rotate customer IP addresses. Although the host name of a slave may resolve to the correct IP address for many weeks, one day the slave may have a new IP address. If this happens, it will not be permitted to access the master. A bad SQL statement in the binary log could cause a slave to stop replicating. If a table is removed or renamed from the slave by an administrator, it would cause an error next time there's a change to that table on the master.

For whatever reason a slave might stop replicating, it won't ring an alarm bell to tell you it has failed. As administrator, you will need to check regularly that the slave is running. In this chapter I will explain a few ways that you could do this. However, since the state should be checked often and regularly, you might want to set up a script which will do this for you. In this short chapter I present a couple of ways in which you might develop a script or program which will check the slave to make sure it's running.

Basic Manual Monitoring

There are several basic methods for checking a slave to see if it's replicating properly. I've touched on them in other chapters. However, this chapter on monitoring replication warrants more details on the essential methods.

Slave Status

The SQL statement, SHOW SLAVE STATUS is the most informative way to check the slave. In the results, look for the Slave_IO_Running and the Slave_SQL_Running fields. If they say, Yes, the slave is running. The first field, Slave_IO_State will tell you about the situation between the master and the slave. If the slave is not running or there's a problem, the last four fields (Last_IO_Errno, Last_IO_Error, Last_SQL_Errno, Last_SQL_Error) will show the last errors received for the slave's two replication threads.

Compare Positions with Master

Another method for checking replication is to compare the slave's position in the master's binary log to that of the master's position in its binary log. To do this, execute this SQL statement on the master:

Example 9.1: Checking Master Status

```
SHOW MASTER STATUS \G
****************** 1. row ******************
         File: binary_log.000081
     Position: 302839126
 Binlog_Do_DB:
```

Basic Manual Monitoring

Binlog_Ignore_DB:

This shows you the name of the current binary log on the master (*binary_log.000081* in this example) and its position in the log (*302839126* here). Next run SHOW SLAVE STATUS on the slave. Look for the fields Master_Log_File and Read_Master_Log_Pos. If the values of these fields equal their equivalents on the master, then the slave is synchronized with the master. This isn't a flawless test, though. If the master is very active and users make changes often, the results between the master and slave may vary slightly. However, if the slave shows an IO state which says, "*Waiting for master to send event,*" the position in the master's binary log should be the same on both servers.

Master Processes

Another method similar to the previous one in this list would be to execute the SHOW PROCESSLIST on the master. This will tell you the state of the slave from the master's point of view. That SQL statement, though, will list all processes on the master. For an active server, the list may be quite long. Unfortunately, the SHOW PROCESSLIST statement doesn't allow for a WHERE clause so as to display only the replication user account's process. Instead, you can get the specific process you want by going to the table where it's stored, PROCESSLIST in the information_schema database. You would execute the following SQL statement on the master:

Basic Manual Monitoring

Example 9.2: Check Process for Slave on Master

```
SELECT * FROM information_schema.processlist
WHERE user = 'replicant' \G

*************** 1. row ***************
     ID: 154766
   USER: replicant
   HOST: slave_host:46784
     DB: NULL
COMMAND: Binlog Dump
   TIME: 86697
  STATE: Has sent all binlog to slave;
         waiting for binlog to be updated
   INFO: NULL
```

If the value in the State field says, "*Has sent all binlog to slave; waiting for binlog to be updated,*" then when you run SHOW SLAVE STATUS on the slave, the value for Slave_IO_State should say "*Waiting for master to send event.*" Basically, the state on the master should correspond to the state of the slave if they're communicating properly.

Automated Methods

While the methods described thus far can be useful in spot checking a server, you may want to be notified that a slave stopped replicating as soon after it happens as possible. To do this, you will need to set up some automated methods of checking the slave to see if replication is running. The reminder of this chapter presents some script and program examples which will do this.

Automated Methods

Just Checking

Below is a simple bash shell script which will check if replication is running on the slave. It will run check the value of the MySQL variable `Slave_Running` in the `information_schema` database. It will send the administrator an email message saying if the slave is not running. You could have a scheduler program like `crontab` start this run this for you each day.

Code Example 9.1: Slave Running Check

```bash
#!/bin/bash

admin='russell'
subject='Replication Status'

sql=" SELECT variable_value "
sql+="FROM information_schema.global_status "
sql+="WHERE variable_name = 'slave_running';"

state=`echo $sql|mysql --user=adm --password=pwd -ss`

if [ $state = 'ON' ]; then
    echo 'Slave is Running'
elif [ $state='OFF' ]; then
    message='Slave is Not Running'
else
    message='Script Failed'
fi

echo $message|mail -s "$subject" "$admin"
```

This script only checks if the slave is running. If it's not running, you might want to know the replication state of the slave and if the slave has experienced any errors. Unfortunately, MySQL doesn't store this information in a a variable that may be retrieved easily. Instead, you have to run the SHOW SLAVE STATUS statement and read the results.

Chapter 9: Monitoring Replication, 93

Code Example 9.1: Slave Running Check

More Details

To be able to extract the values of only certain fields of the results table from the SQL statement SHOW SLAVE STATUS, you will need a more complicated script than the previous one. For this, I prefer a programming language like Perl. Below is a sample Perl program that I wrote which does this:

Code Example 9.2: Slave Status Report

```perl
#!/usr/bin/perl -w
use strict;
use DBI;

my $user = 'replication_admin';
my $pwd = 'its_pwd';
my $host = 'localhost';
my $dbh = DBI->connect("DBI:mysql:test;host=$host;
                       user=$user;password=$pwd",
                       undef, undef, {RaiseError=>1});

my $sql_stmnt = q|SHOW SLAVE STATUS|;
my $sth = $dbh->prepare($sql_stmnt);
$sth->execute();
my @slave_status = $sth->fetchrow_array();
$sth->finish();
$dbh->disconnect();

my ($slave_io_state) = $slave_status[0];
my ($slave_io_running) = $slave_status[10];
my ($slave_sql_running) = $slave_status[11];
my ($last_io_errno) = $slave_status[34];
my ($last_io_error) = $slave_status[35];
my ($last_sql_errno) = $slave_status[36];
my ($last_sql_error) = $slave_status[37];

print 'Slave Status', "\n",
      '---------------------------', "\n",
      'Slave_IO_State: ', $slave_io_state, "\n",
      'Slave_IO_Running: ', $slave_io_running, "\n",
      'Last_IO_Errno: ', $last_io_errno, "\n",
      'Last_IO_Error: ', $last_io_error, "\n",
      'Slave_SQL_Running; ', $slave_sql_running, "\n",
      'Last_SQL_Errno: ', $last_sql_errno, "\n",
      'Last_SQL_Error: ', $last_sql_error, "\n\n";
```

```
                                    exit;
```

Here are the results of this Perl program:

Example 9.3:   Perl Program Results

```
Slave Status
---------------------------
Slave_IO_State: Waiting for master to send event
Slave_IO_Running: Yes
Last_IO_Errno: 0
Last_IO_Error:
Slave_SQL_Running; Yes
Last_SQL_Errno: 0
Last_SQL_Error:
```

This program is very minimal. It has no error checking and has no concerns for security. It's dependent on the field of the results set of SHOW SLAVE STATUS, not changing their order. Also, it's only designed to display the information when executed. You could modify it to mail you the text in a message like the previous bash script does. I'll leave it to you to create the program and method that works for you. I'm just providing you with examples and ideas about how you might accomplish what you need to be effective as an administrator.

Data Comparison

Although it may be unnecessary on most slaves, you may want to spot check the data on the slaves to ensure replication is working properly. When there has been a major outage and especially if you have had difficulty re-establishing replication, you may want at

Code Example 9.2: Slave Status Report

least to do some simple checks. For instance, you might use the function COUNT( ) to count the number of rows in large tables on both the master and the slave. You might use SUM( ) to add up the values of integer columns and compare the totals from the master to the slave. If you get different results, you might have lost some data somewhere—it could just be that data has changed on the master only a couple of seconds before you checked the slave. You might have to get a read lock on both servers first.

If you determine that there are data discrepancies, which may be a rare occurrence, you may want to start over with replication by making another full back-up of the master's databases and replacing all of the databases and data on the slave.

Below is a Perl program I wrote for making bulk comparisons between the master and slave databases. The program extracts two simple statistics from the master and from the slave for each database and table: the number of rows of each table and the size of each table. After it extracts this data from each server, it saves the data in a temporary table for comparison. It displays a list of databases and tables that either don't have the same number of rows, or tables which are not the same size. If your servers are running on different operating systems (i.e., Linux and FreeBSD), the byte count may always be different. In that kind of a scenario, you may want to eliminate the byte count comparison.

Code Example 9.3: Master & Slave Comparison

```perl
#!/usr/bin/perl -w
use strict;
use DBI;

# Connect to Slave
my $user_slave = 'myadmin';
my $pwd_slave = 'its_pwd';
my $connect_str_slave = qq|DBI:mysql:information_schema;|
                      . qq|host=localhost;|
                      . qq|user=$user_slave;|
                      . qq|password=$pwd_slave|;
my $dbh_slave = DBI->connect($connect_str_slave,
                             undef, undef,
                             {RaiseError=>1})
              || die 'Could Not Connect to Slave: '
                   . DBI->errstr;

# Connect to Master
my $host_master = 'master_hos';
my $user_master = 'myadmin';
my $pwd_master = 'its_pwd';
my $connect_str_master = qq|DBI:mysql:information_schema;|
                       . qq|host=$host_master;|
                       . qq|user=$user_master;|
                       . qq|password=$pwd_master|;
my $dbh_master = DBI->connect($connect_str_master,
                              undef, undef,
                              {RaiseError=>1})
               || die 'Could Not Connect to Master: '
                    . DBI->errstr;

# Create Temporary Tables for Stats
my $sql_stmnt = q|CREATE TEMPORARY TABLE
                  test.compare_master
                  (database_name VARCHAR(255),
                   table_name VARCHAR(255),
                   row_count INT, data_length INT,
                   size_type
                   ENUM('table','database','server'))|;
$dbh_slave->do($sql_stmnt, undef, undef);

$sql_stmnt = q|CREATE TEMPORARY TABLE
               test.comparison_slave
               (database_name VARCHAR(255),
                table_name VARCHAR(255),
                row_count INT, data_length INT,
                size_type
                ENUM('table','database','server'))|;
```

Code Example 9.3: Master & Slave Comparison

```perl
$dbh_slave->do($sql_stmnt, undef, undef);

# Assemble Data and Process
my $table_stats = get_table_row_counts($dbh_master);
&process_table_stats('master',$table_stats);
$table_stats = get_table_row_counts($dbh_slave);
&process_table_stats('slave',$table_stats);

# Report Server Comparison
my ($row_diff,$size_diff) = &get_svr_diff();
my ($row_label,$size_label) = &get_labels($row_diff,
$size_diff);

print "Replication Server: \n",
      abs($row_diff), $row_label,
      abs($size_diff), $size_label, "\n",
      "=========================================\n";


# Report Each Database Comparison
my $db_diff = &get_db_diff();

foreach (@$db_diff) {
  my ($db_name,$row_diff,$size_diff) = @$_;
  my ($row_label,$size_label) = &get_labels($row_diff,
$size_diff);

  print "\nDatabase: ", $database_name, "\n",
        abs($row_diff), $row_label,
        abs($size_diff), $size_label, "\n",
        "----------------------------------------\n";

  # Report Table Comparisons for Database
  my $table_diff = &get_table_diff($database_name);

  foreach (@$table_diff) {
    my ($table_name,$row_diff,$size_diff) = @$_;
    my ($row_label,$size_label) = &get_labels($row_diff,
$size_diff);

    print $table_name, ': ',
          abs($row_diff), $row_label,
          abs($size_diff), $size_label, "\n";
  }
}

# Disconnect and Exit
$dbh_master->disconnect();
$dbh_slave->disconnect();
```

Code Example 9.3: Master & Slave Comparison

```perl
exit;

sub get_db_diff {
  # Compare Stat Totals for Databases on Master to
Databases on Slave
  $sql_stmnt = qq|SELECT slave.database_name,
                    master.row_count - slave.row_count
                      AS row_diff,
                    master.data_length - slave.data_length
                      AS size_diff
                    FROM test.comparison_master AS master
                    JOIN test.comparison_slave AS slave
                    USING(database_name, table_name)
                    WHERE master.size_type = 'database'
                    AND master.row_count != slave.row_count
                    OR master.size_type = 'database'
                    AND master.data_length !=
slave.data_length|;
  my $sth = $dbh_slave->prepare($sql_stmnt);
  $sth->execute();
  my $db_diff = $sth->fetchall_arrayref();
  $sth->finish();

  return $db_diff;
}

sub get_svr_diff {
  # Compare Stats for All Databases on Master to Slave
  $sql_stmnt = qq|SELECT master.row_count - slave.row_count
                      AS row_diff,
                    master.data_length - slave.data_length
                      AS size_diff
                    FROM test.comparison_master AS master
                    JOIN test.comparison_slave AS slave
                    USING(database_name, table_name)
                    WHERE master.size_type = 'server'
                    AND master.row_count != slave.row_count
                    OR master.size_type = 'server'
                    AND master.data_length !=
slave.data_length|;
  my $sth = $dbh_slave->prepare($sql_stmnt);
  $sth->execute();
  my ($row_diff,$size_diff) = $sth->fetchrow_array();
  $sth->finish();

  return ($row_diff,$size_diff);
}
```

Code Example 9.3: Master & Slave Comparison

```perl
sub get_table_diff {
  # Compare Stats for Tables for a given Database in Master
  # to the same Tables in Slave
  my $db_name = shift;

  $sql_stmnt = qq|SELECT slave.table_name,
                  master.row_count - slave.row_count
                    AS row_diff,
                  master.data_length - slave.data_length
                    AS size_diff
                  FROM test.comparison_master AS master
                  JOIN test.comparison_slave AS slave
                  USING(db_name, table_name)
                  WHERE master.size_type = 'table'
                  AND slave.db_name = ?
                  AND master.row_count != slave.row_count
                  OR master.size_type = 'table'
                  AND slave.db_name = ?
                  AND master.data_length !=
slave.data_length|;
  my $sth = $dbh_slave->prepare($sql_stmnt);
  $sth->execute($db_name,$db_name);
  my $table_diff = $sth->fetchall_arrayref();
  $sth->finish();

  return $table_diff;
}

sub get_table_row_counts {
  # Get List of Tables and Number of Rows in Each
  my $dbh = shift;
  $sql_stmnt = q|SELECT table_schema, table_name,
                  SUM(table_rows), SUM(data_length)
                  FROM tables
                  WHERE table_schema NOT IN
                  ('information_schema','mysql','test')
                  GROUP BY table_schema, table_name
                  WITH ROLLUP|;
  my $sth = $dbh->prepare($sql_stmnt);
  $sth->execute();
  my $table_stats = $sth->fetchall_arrayref();
  $sth->finish();
  return $table_stats;
}

sub get_values_labels {
  # Set Value Labels
  my ($row_diff,$size_diff) = @_;
  my $row_label = ' more rows, ';
  my $size_label = ' bytes more';
```

Code Example 9.3: Master & Slave Comparison

```perl
  if($row_diff lt 0) {
     $row_label = ' less rows, ';
  }
  if($size_diff lt 0) {
     $size_label = ' bytes less';
  }

  return ($row_label,$size_label);
}
sub process_table_stats {
  # Loop through List of Tables for Each Server
  my ($server_type,$table_stats) = @_;

  foreach (@$table_stats) {
    my ($db_name,$tbl_name,$row_count,$data_length) = @$_;
    &save_to_temp_table($server_type,$db_name,$tbl_name,
$row_count,$data_length);
  }
}
sub save_to_temp_table {
  # Save Results to Temporary Table in MySQL
  my ($compare_table,$db_name,$tbl_name,$row_count,
$data_length) = @_;

  if($compare_table eq 'master') {
     $compare_table = 'comparison_master';
  }
  else {
     $compare_table = 'comparison_slave';
  }

  my $size_type = 'table';
  if(!$db_name) {
     ($db_name,$tbl_name,$size_type) = ('','','server')
  }
  elsif(!$tbl_name) {
     ($tbl_name,$size_type) = ('','database')
  }

  $sql_stmnt = qq|INSERT INTO test.$compare_table
                  SET db_name = ?, table_name = ?,
                  row_count = ?, data_length = ?,
                  size_type = ?|;
  my $sth = $dbh_slave->prepare($sql_stmnt);
  $sth->execute($db_name,$tbl_name,$row_count,$data_length,
$size_type);
  $sth->finish();
```

Code Example 9.3: Master & Slave Comparison

}

An Alternative

Some of the people from MySQL have started a new community project for monitoring replication. It's called simply, the *MySQL Community Replication Monitor*. It's GPL software, a set of scripts for monitoring MySQL Replication. It's a very new project, but you may find it useful. Its web address is *http://launchpad.net/mysql-replication-monitor.*

Chapter 10
Load Balancing

Besides using replication so as to have a back-up server running continuously and to be able to make copies of such back-up servers more easily, MySQL Replication can be used to spread the load of user activities between the slave servers. Instead of one MySQL server responding to user requests for data, with replication you can set up multiple slave servers, each providing users with data. Slave servers can even be placed in different locations to protect against system outages.

Load balancing can be handled by a few methods. It's a complex topic and a bit beyond the scope of a short book such as this. However, I will attempt to provide some basic information on how it may be accomplished, especially for databases that do not have an overly large volume of users.

Factors to Consider

There are a few things to consider when deciding on how loads should be spread between servers. Ideally, a load balancing replication scheme should be set up so that users are always able to get a connection and they are unaware that load balancing is going on, so that they don't have to do anything differently based on load activities. For instance, it's not seamless to require users to click on a different web page link if one server is busy so as to select another server.

With load balancing, you might not necessarily want to balance user activities between slave servers equally, but rather appropriately between resources. For example, if one slave server has much greater bandwidth than another, equal distribution of user requests will cause one server to be under used and another to be strained, with its users experiencing slow responses. So, if possible, you should try to use slaves, efficiently. Along these lines, you should set up your replication and load balancing system so that you can easily add or remove servers.

The ability to add slaves and balance accordingly can be useful when something occurs that causes user activities to increase tremendously and rapidly. Being able to remove servers without a noticeable loss of service to users, with the load easily or automatically adjusting itself is handy for when you need to remove a slave from replication so that you can do some maintenance or just to make a back-up.

One important factor is to make sure that related transactions are performed on the same server for consistency of data. This is particularly important when a user is changing or adding data to MySQL.

Simple Load Balancing Method

You could purchase expensive hardware designed for load balancing or buy high-end, slick software to handle the balancing of your system's load. However, if you don't have the money or desire to go these routes, you will have to look for simpler methods to work with what you have. The easiest inexpensive way to balance user activities between MySQL servers is to restrict read-only requests to the slaves and reserve the master server for data changes. For many MySQL databases, the public has only read-only access. So this method of organizing MySQL Replication servers is just fine for them: employees making changes to the master and customers using several slave servers.

Directing based on SQL Statement

To direct reads to slave servers and writes to the master server, you will need to make modifications to your applications. So if you have a set of PHP or Perl scripts or other applications that interface user web pages to MySQL databases, you will need to edit them. Basically, you will have different connect statements (e.g., `mysql_connect( )` in PHP, specifying a different server; `connect( )` in Perl, specifying a different host) depending on whether a connection is being used to read

Directing based on SQL Statement

(e.g., the SQL statement used by a script is a `SELECT` statement) or to write (e.g., the SQL statement used includes an `INSERT` or an `UPDATE`) data to a database.

For some read requests it may be important that the user have current data. For these user requests, you may want to send them to the master server along with write requests.

Checking Age of Data

Once you start trying to decide which queries within your applications need to read current data, you may end up becoming overly cautious and send almost all read requests to the master, defeating your load balancing plans. To keep this to a minimum, you can check the slave server to see if it was updated recently. If it was, then your application can use its data. If the data is a bit stale, you can direct the user (or application) request to the master. You will have to set up a notation in a table in MySQL on the slave server as to when data was last updated and then set a policy for the server to decide how old is too old for the slave to be used. This approach can be very important when replication has stopped—especially when it stops without you knowing. Otherwise, users could be reading very old data and not realize it.

Considering Age for Writers

As mentioned before, replication works best when the user doesn't experience any lags in data requests—or at least when the user is unaware of it. If a user changes data on the master server, probably other users will be unaware of it until the slave server from which they're reading gets the update. If replication is running well, there should only be a few seconds of a delay, at most. The only user that will notice the delay will be the one who has just added or changed the data. Many web sites will simply inform the user that their changes will not appear immediately. This may not be as seamless as you might want. So, you could make adjustments for such a situation.

For a user who has written recently to the master server, you could direct all subsequent read requests from that user to the master until the slave has synchronized again. To do this, you will need to adjust your applications, maybe create a table in MySQL to which you note the time of the last write by the user. Then you would just compare this time to the time that one of the slave servers was last synchronized to decide when to direct the user's subsequent requests to that slave. Stick to one slave for comparison and subsequent use until the time of the slave exceeds that of the user's write. If you instead send the user to another slave server, it might not have been synchronized yet: this would defeat the tweak to your load balancing scheme.

Other Methods

There are other methods by which you can balance a MySQL server's load between slave servers. For instance, you could use domain name service (DNS) to spread the load between servers. You could also use virtual IP addresses, similarly. However, these methods aren't very effective—they aren't especially reliable. If you'd like to use software that don't require you to modify your applications, consider the software *Wackamole*. You can find it on the web at this address: http://www.backhand.org/wackamole/. Another software option is to use Linux Virtual Server. See their knowledge base for information: http://kb.linuxvirtualserver.org/wiki/Load_balancer.

A final recommendation, which may be the best of the low cost methods, is to use *MySQL Proxy*, a new product from MySQL. It's a simple program that acts as a go-between for clients and MySQL servers. Basically, it monitors and directs client traffic. This includes load balancing, server failover, query analysis, and query filtering. These are the features I mentioned that you might build into your own applications, the features for which you should be striving with MySQL Replication and load balancing. Best of all, MySQL Proxy is free since it's released under the GPL. The only drawback at this point is that it's still a new product in its early stages and may not yet be fully bug free or be able to offer you everything you need. This is why you might do better by modifying your own applications, to get exactly what you need. Still, you probably should check out *MySQL Proxy*. You can get more information on it from their web site at http://forge.mysql.com/wiki/MySQL_Proxy.

Appendixes

Three appendixes are included in this book. In fact, one might think this book to be heavy in appendixes considering the number of pages in the appendixes compared to the rest of the book. However, the information provided in the appendixes may prove useful in administering replication servers. In a sense, this is two books bound together as one. The first book, the chapters, is a tutorial on understanding and setting up MySQL Replication, as well as setting up back-ups using replication. The second book, the appendixes, is a reference manual of various aspects of replication and SQL statements and utilities related to MySQL Replication.

Appendix A contains a list of SQL statements and functions in MySQL which are specifically or primarily used with MySQL Replication. Appendix B lists all MySQL Replication states and describes each. These are particularly useful in resolving problems related to a stalled replication system. Appendix C contains a quick reference of command-line utilities that are mentioned in the chapters of this book and are often used when running replication. These pages are mostly confined to replication options or replication aspects of the utilities.

Appendix A
SQL Statements & Functions

Several SQL statements apply directly to replication. One function, `MASTER_POS_WAIT( )`, also applies to replication, and is listed alphabetically here with the SQL statements. The basic format for each is to present the statement and its syntax along with some minor details regarding the required user permissions and other factors. These items are followed by an explanation of each and examples of how they might be used.

CHANGE MASTER TO

Syntax:
```
CHANGE MASTER TO
[MASTER_HOST = 'host' |
 MASTER_USER = 'user' |
 MASTER_PASSWORD = 'password' |
 MASTER_PORT = port |
 MASTER_CONNECT_RETRY = count |
 MASTER_LOG_FILE = 'filename' |
 MASTER_LOG_POS = position |
 RELAY_LOG_FILE = 'filename' |
 RELAY_LOG_POS = position |
 MASTER_SSL = {0|1} |
 MASTER_SSL_CA = 'filename' |
 MASTER_SSL_CAPATH = 'path' |
 MASTER_SSL_CERT = 'filename' |
 MASTER_SSL_KEY = 'filename' |
 MASTER_SSL_CIPHER = 'list' |
 MASTER_SSL_VERIFY_SERVER_CERT =
    {0|1}], [,...]
```

Permissions: SUPER
Server: Slave

Version Notes:
RELAY_LOG_FILE: 4.1.1
RELAY_LOG_POS: 4.1.1
MASTER_SSL_VERIFY_SERVER_CERT: 5.1.18

This statement changes the settings on a slave server related to the master server and replication. Some of the variables relate to connecting to the master server and some relate to master log files and the current position in the log files. It's run from the slave.

If the slave is busy replicating, it may be necessary to use the STOP SLAVE statement before using this statement and the START SLAVE statement afterward. These options can be set from the server's options file, but it's much better to use this SQL statement to set MySQL Replication options since changes are immediate with this it.

CHANGE MASTER TO

Multiple options and value pairs may be given in one CHANGE MASTER TO statement, as long as the pairs are separated by commas. Below is an example of this SQL statement. It sets several properties on the slave for connecting to the master.

```
CHANGE MASTER TO
   MASTER_HOST='mysql.somecompany.com',
   MASTER_PORT=3306,
   MASTER_USER='slave_server',
   MASTER_PASSWORD='its_pwd',
   MASTER_CONNECT_RETRY=5;
```

Once this statement is executed, these values are saved to the master.info file, including the password. All of these values except for the password can be retrieved from the SHOW SLAVE STATUS statement. To retrieve the password, you will have to open the master.info file.

Looking back at the syntax possibilities you will see clauses related to log files. They set the master log files and provide the slave with the current position of the master log files. This may be necessary when first setting up a new slave or when a slave has been disabled for a while. Use the SHOW MASTER STATUS statement to determine the current position of the master log files, and the SHOW SLAVE STATUS statement to confirm a slave's position for the related files. Here is an example using the clauses related to log files:

```
CHANGE MASTER TO
   MASTER_LOG_FILE= 'log-bin.000153',
   MASTER_LOG_POS = 79,
   RELAY_LOG_FILE = 'log-relay.000153',
   RELAY_LOG_POS = 112;
```

Appendix A: SQL Statements & Functions, 113

CHANGE MASTER TO

The remaining clauses for the CHANGE MASTER TO statement set various secure socket layer (SSL) variables. These values are saved to the `master.info` file. To see the current values for these options, use the SHOW SLAVE STATUS statement.

The MASTER_SSL variable is set to 0 if the master does not allow SSL connections, and 1 if it does. The MASTER_SSL_CA variable holds the name of the file that contains a list of trusted Cas. MASTER_SSL_CAPATH contains the absolute path to that file. The MASTER_SSL_CERT variable specifies the name of the SSL certificate file for secure connections, and MASTER_SSL_KEY specifies the SSL key file used to negotiate secure connections. Finally, MASTER_SSL_CIPHER provides a list of acceptable cipher methods for encryption.

LOAD DATA FROM MASTER

Syntax:
LOAD DATA FROM MASTER

Deprecated

Permissions:
On Master, RELOAD, SELECT, & SUPER
On Slave, CREATE & DROP

Server: Slave

This SQL statement has been deprecated and will be removed from future releases of MySQL. It never worked very well. It was meant to make a copy of all of the databases on the master server (except the *mysql*

LOAD DATA FROM MASTER

database) and copy them to the slave servers. It gets a global read lock on all tables while it takes a snapshot of the databases, and releases the lock before copying them to the slaves. The `MASTER_LOG_FILE` and `MASTER_LOG_POS` variables will be updated so that the slave knows where to begin logging.

This statement works only with MyISAM tables. For tables for other storage engines, Error 1189 is returned with the message, "*Net error reading from master.*" For large databases, increase the values of the `net_read_timeout` and `net_write_timeout` variables with the `SET` statement. To load a specific table from the master server, use the `LOAD TABLE...FROM MASTER` statement.

Again, this statement does not work very well: it's not dependable and usually has problems with properly copying data from the master to the slave. Instead, use a utility such as `mysqldump` to copy the data on the master and then transfer the resulting file to the slave, as described in Chapter 4, *Copying the Initial Data*.

LOAD TABLE...FROM MASTER

Syntax:
    LOAD TABLE table FROM MASTER

Deprecated
Permissions:
On Master, RELOAD, SELECT, & SUPER
On Slave, CREATE & DROP

Server: Slave

This statement has been deprecated and will be removed from future releases of MySQL since it has many problems. It was meant for copying a MyISAM table from the master server to a slave server.

Instead of using this statement, use a utility like `mysqldump` to copy the data from the master. Then copy the export file created by `mysqldump` to the slave and load it into the slave with the client `mysql`. This method is described in Chapter 4, *Copying the Initial Data*.

MASTER_POS_WAIT( )

Syntax:
    MASTER_POS_WAIT(log_filename, log_position[, timeout])

Permissions: SUPER
Server: Slave

Version Notes:
5.1.42 generates warning since unsafe for statement-based replication

This is a function and it's a useful tool for synchronizing MySQL master and slave server logs. The function causes the master to wait until the slave server has read and applied all updates to a specific position (given in the second argument) in the master log (named in the first argument). You can specify optionally a third argument to set the number of seconds the master should wait. A value of 0 or a negative amount is given to instruct the master not to time out and to keep waiting. This function may cause problems if your binary log is set to statement-based replication.

The function returns the number of log entries that were made by the slave while the master was waiting. If all is set properly, you should receive these results, rapidly. However, if there is an error, NULL is returned. NULL is also returned if the slave's SQL thread is not started, if the slave's master options are not set, or if the parameters given with this function are not correct. If you give the timeout parameter and the amount of time is exceeded, -1 is returned.

PURGE MASTER LOGS

Syntax:
```
PURGE {MASTER|BINARY} LOGS
   {TO 'log_filename'|BEFORE 'date'}
```

Permissions: SUPER
Server: Slave
Version Notes:
5.1.24, no problems; synonymous with PURGE BINARY LOGS

This statement deletes the binary logs from a master server. The keywords MASTER and BINARY are synonymous; one is required for the statement. Log files are deleted sequentially from the starting log file until the one named with the TO clause, or up until (but not including) the date named with the BEFORE clause. Here is an example of each method:

```
PURGE MASTER LOGS TO 'log-bin.00110';
PURGE MASTER LOGS BEFORE '2009-11-03 07:00:00';
```

PURGE MASTER LOGS

Before running this statement, it would be prudent to make a back-up of the logs. Then use `SHOW SLAVE STATUS` on each slave to determine which logs the slaves are reading, and run `SHOW BINARY LOGS` on the master server to get a list of log files. The oldest log file in the list is the one that will be purged. If the slaves are current, they shouldn't be reading this log file. If they still are, you may not want to purge it. If you find that your log files aren't being rotated very often, you can set the system variable `expire_logs_days` to shorten the amount of time before new log files are created and old ones archived. This will also help to keep log files from becoming excessively large.

RESET MASTER

Syntax:
`RESET MASTER`

Permissions: SUPER
Server: Slave

This statement deletes all of the binary log files on the master server. Binary log files are located in the directory indicated by the value of the `--log-bin` option of `mysqld`, usually listed in the options file. The log files are typically named `log-bin.index`, where *index* is a six-digit numbering index. Use the `SHOW MASTER LOGS` statement to get a list of log files to be sure.

RESET MASTER

When this statement is executed, after deleting all of the master log files, a new log file will be created, with the new file suffix of `000001`. To get the slave servers in line with the reset master, run the `RESET SLAVE` statement. You can run the `MASTER` and `SLAVE` options together in a comma-separated list like so:

```
RESET MASTER, SLAVE;
```

This is a recommended method for ensuring consistency between the slaves and the master.

RESET SLAVE

Syntax:
`RESET SLAVE`

Permissions: SUPER
Server: Slave

Use this statement within or after the `RESET MASTER` statement that sets the binary logging index back to `000001`. This statement will delete the `master.info` file, the `relay-log.info` file, and all of the relay log files on the slave server. It will delete the relay log files regardless of whether the SQL thread has finished executing its contents—so be careful using it. A new pair of `.info` files and a new relay log file will be created with the default, start-up values.

SET GLOBAL SQL_SLAVE_SKIP_COUNTER

Syntax:
SET GLOBAL
 SQL_SLAVE_SKIP_COUNTER = *number*

Permissions: SUPER
Server: Slave

This SQL statement tells the slave to skip the given number of events from the master. It's used for fine tuning a recovery. For instance, there may be a set of SQL statements in the binary log that causes the slave to stop replicating. With this SQL statement here, you can tell the slave to skip the statements that are causing the problem. It returns an error if the slave thread is running. So you will need to stop replication on the slave first.

```
STOP SLAVE;
SET GLOBAL SQL_SLAVE_SKIP_COUNTER=10;
START SLAVE;
```

A replication event is generally an SQL statement or other activity logged in the binary log. Such events can be grouped together, though. For non-transactional storage engines (e.g., MyISAM), an event group is composed only of a single SQL statement in the binary log. However, for transactional storage engines (e.g., InnoDB), a transaction—which can include multiple SQL statements—is considered a single replication event group. If you tell the slave to skip a certain number of events and the last requested event would put the slave in a position of executing SQL statements beginning from the middle of a transaction, it will instead skip to the end of the event group in which it finds itself. To do otherwise would probably cause problems with the data.

SET SQL_LOG_BIN

Syntax:
```
SET SQL_LOG_BIN = {0|1}
```

Permissions: SUPER
Server: Master

This statement enables or disables binary logging of SQL statements for the current session of a client. It does not affect logging for the activities of other sessions and is reset to the default value when the client session is closed. The statement requires SUPER privileges. A value of 0 disables binary logging; 1 enables it.

```
SET SQL_LOG_BIN = 0;
```

This can be a covert SQL statement. It can allow a user to enter SQL statements on the master and their activities would not be logged. It can be legitimately useful, though, if you want to make changes on the master, but don't want those changes replicated on the slaves. When used to disable binary logging, it only disables it for the current connection; it's not a global setting.

SHOW BINLOG EVENTS

Syntax:
```
SHOW BINLOG EVENTS
[IN 'log_filename']
[FROM position]
[LIMIT [offset,] count]
```

Permissions: SUPER
Server: Master

This statement displays the events in a binary log file. Use the IN clause to specify a particular log file. If the IN clause is omitted, the current file is used. To obtain a

SHOW BINLOG EVENTS

list of binary log files, use the `SHOW MASTER LOGS` statement. Here is an example of how you can use this statement and typical results:

```
SHOW BINLOG EVENTS IN 'log-bin.000161' \G
************ 1. row ************
   Log_name: log-bin.000161
        Pos: 4
 Event_type: Start
  Server_id: 1
Orig_log_pos: 4
       Info: Server ver: 5.1.41-log, Binlog ver: 3
1 row in set (0.00 sec)
```

This log file has only one row of data, because the SQL statement was run shortly after the server was started. For a larger log file recording many rows of events, the results take a long time and drain system resources significantly. To minimize this you can focus and limit the results with the FROM and LIMIT clauses. In the results above, notice that the *Pos* label has a value of 4. In a large log file, that number might be in the thousands. The results displayed could be focused only on rows starting from a particular position in the log with the FROM clause. You can limit the number of rows of events displayed with the LIMIT clause. In the LIMIT clause, you can also set the starting point of the output based on the number of rows in the results set and limit them to a certain number of rows. Here is an example of both of these clauses:

```
SHOW BINLOG EVENTS IN 'log-bin.000160'
FROM 3869 LIMIT 2,1\G
************ 1. row ************
   Log_name: log-bin.000160
        Pos: 4002
```

```
     Event_type: Intvar
      Server_id: 1
  Orig_log_pos: 4002
           Info: INSERT_ID=5
```

In this example, the retrieval of log events is to begin from position 3869 because of the `FROM` clause. The results set contains several rows, although only one is shown here. The display is limited to one row, starting from the third one in the results set per the `LIMIT` clause. The number of skipped records is the sum of the `FROM` argument and the first `LIMIT` argument.

As an alternative to using this statement when working with large binary log files, you might try using the `mysqlbinlog` utility and redirecting the results to a text file that you can read in a text editor when it's finished. Besides, this utility will provide you more information than `SHOW BINLOG EVENTS`.

SHOW MASTER LOGS

Syntax:
   SHOW {BINARY|MASTER} LOGS

Permissions: SUPER
Server: Slave

This statement displays a list of binary logs created by the master server along with the file system directory where they're located. The keywords `MASTER` and `BINARY` are synonymous for this SQL statement, but one is required, of course. Below is an example of this statement and the results it returns:

SHOW MASTER LOGS

```
SHOW MASTER LOGS;

+--------------------+------------+
| Log_name           | File_size  |
+--------------------+------------+
| binary_log.000001  |   11371268 |
| binary_log.000002  |   14378985 |
| binary_log.000003  |    2284279 |
| binary_log.000004  |       2077 |
+--------------------+------------+
```

To delete logs, see the description of `PURGE MASTER LOGS` statement. To enable logs, as described in Chapter 3, *Configuring Servers*, use the `--log-bin` option for `mysqld`.

SHOW MASTER STATUS

Syntax:
SHOW MASTER STATUS

Permissions:
SUPER, REPLICATION CLIENT
Server: Master

This SQL statement displays information on the status of the binary log file on the master server. It also shows the current position number from the master of the last replication event that has been executed by the slave. This is not the master's current position number in its own logs, but the slave's bookmark.

```
SHOW MASTER STATUS;

+-------------------+-----------+--------------+------------------+
| File              | Position  | Binlog_Do_DB | Binlog_Ignore_DB |
+-------------------+-----------+--------------+------------------+
| binary_log.000081 | 303563845 |              | mysql, test      |
+-------------------+-----------+--------------+------------------+
```

You'll notice two other fields in these results besides the two already mentioned above. The results show the names of two databases (`mysql` and `test`) listed in the field, `Binlog_Ignore_DB`. The slave has been instructed to ignore events related to these databases, not to replicate them. It's set on the slave with the `--binary-ignore-db` option for `mysqld`. If you want a slave to replicate only certain databases, you could use the `--binlog-do-db` option in `mysqld` on the slave to list the databases. The names of these databases would then appear in the `Binlo_Do_DB` field of the results above.

SHOW SLAVE HOSTS

Syntax:
SHOW SLAVE HOSTS

Permissions: SUPER
Server: Master

This SQL statement displays a list of slave servers for the master server. Slaves must be started with the `--report-host=`*slave* option in order to be shown.

```
SHOW SLAVE HOSTS;
+-----------+-----------+------+-----------+
| Server_id | Host      | Port | Master_id |
+-----------+-----------+------+-----------+
|         2 | slave2    | 3306 |         1 |
|         3 | slave3    | 3306 |         1 |
+-----------+-----------+------+-----------+
```

As you can see, the results returns four fields. `Server_id` is the server identification number for the slave server, which is set by the `--server-id` option, preferably in the slave's options file for `mysqld`. `Host` is the host name of the slave server, which is set by the

SHOW SLAVE HOSTS

`--report-host` option on the slave. `Port` is the port on which the slave is listening for replication. This defaults to 3306, but can be set to a different port with the `CHANGE MASTER TO` statement on the slave. Of course, MySQL on the master server will need to be listening and communicating on the alternative port. So you will need to set `--port` in `mysqld` on the master. `Master_id` is the server identification number of the master. It's set on the master with `--server-id` in `mysqld` and conversely on the slave with the `CHANGE MASTER TO` statement. For more information on these settings, see Chapter 3, *Configuring Servers*.

SHOW SLAVE STATUS

Syntax:
```
SHOW SLAVE STATUS
```

Permissions:
SUPER, REPLICATION CLIENT
Server: Slave

Version Notes:
5.1.20, four Last_xxx_Errxx fields added;

This statement displays information on the slave thread. Here is an example of this statement and its results:

```
SHOW SLAVE STATUS\G
***************** 1. row ******************
          Slave_IO_State: Waiting for master
                          to send event
             Master_Host: master_host.com
             Master_User: replicant
             Master_Port: 3306
           Connect_Retry: 60
         Master_Log_File: binary_log.000081
     Read_Master_Log_Pos: 33275939
          Relay_Log_File: relay.000005
           Relay_Log_Pos: 32178164
   Relay_Master_Log_File: binary_log.000081
```

SHOW SLAVE STATUS

```
            Slave_IO_Running: Yes
           Slave_SQL_Running: Yes
             Replicate_Do_DB:
         Replicate_Ignore_DB:
          Replicate_Do_Table:
      Replicate_Ignore_Table:
     Replicate_Wild_Do_Table:
 Replicate_Wild_Ignore_Table:
                  Last_Errno: 0
                  Last_Error:
                Skip_Counter: 0
         Exec_Master_Log_Pos: 33270860
             Relay_Log_Space: 32737824
             Until_Condition: None
              Until_Log_File:
               Until_Log_Pos: 0
          Master_SSL_Allowed: Yes
          Master_SSL_CA_File: ssl_ca.dat
          Master_SSL_CA_Path: /data/mysql/ssl_ca
             Master_SSL_Cert: ssl_cert.dat
           Master_SSL_Cipher:
              Master_SSL_Key:
       Seconds_Behind_Master: 65
Master_SSL_Verify_Server_Cert: No
               Last_IO_Errno: 0
               Last_IO_Error:
              Last_SQL_Errno: 0
              Last_SQL_Error:
```

You can set some of these values at startup with the MySQL server daemon (`mysqld`). See Chapter 3, *Configuring Servers* and Append C for more information on setting server variables at start-up. You can also set some of these variables with the SET statement, and you can adjust others with the CHANGE MASTER TO statement. You can reset some of the log file variables with the RESET MASTER and RESET SLAVE statements.

START SLAVE

Syntax:
```
START SLAVE [IO_THREAD|SQL_THREAD]

START SLAVE [SQL_THREAD]
UNTIL
MASTER_LOG_FILE = 'log_filename',
MASTER_LOG_POS = position

START SLAVE [SQL_THREAD]
UNTIL
RELAY_LOG_FILE = 'log_filename',
RELAY_LOG_POS = position
```

Permissions: SUPER
Server: Slave

Version Notes:
Was SLAVE START before 4.0.5

Use this statement on a slave server to start replication. In the first syntax, you can start just the I/O thread or just the SQL thread by using the respective keyword. You can start both by listing both keywords, separated by a comma. However, the default (i.e., with neither `IO_THREAD` nor `SQL_THREAD` given) will start both threads.

The I/O thread reads SQL queries from the master server and records them in the relay log file. The SQL thread reads the relay log file and then executes the SQL statements it contains. See Chapter 1, *MySQL Replication Process* for details on this process.

The second syntax limits the reading of the threads to a specific point, given with `MASTER_LOG_POS`, in the master log file named with the `MASTER_LOG_FILE` parameter. The `UNTIL` clause stops processing of the given log files when the given position is reached.

START SLAVE

The third syntax specifies the relay log file and limits the reading and execution of its contents. If the `SQL_THREAD` keyword is given in either the second or third syntax, the reading will be limited to the SQL thread.

The starting of a slave thread isn't always dependable. Or rather, you won't be informed if replication stops immediately upon starting it. Therefore, run the `SHOW SLAVE STATUS` statement and look for the value of the variables, `Slave_IO_Running` and `Slave_SQL_Running` to confirm that the threads began and continued running. Both should have a value of `Yes` if you started both.

STOP SLAVE

Syntax:
`STOP SLAVE [IO_THREAD|SQL_THREAD]`

Permissions: SUPER
Server: Slave

Version Notes:
Before 5.1.35, stopped immediately; Now stops after current event group executed—or KILL QUERY or KILL CONNECTION executed

This statement stops the slave server threads. To stop a specific slave thread, specify one or both threads. Both may be given in a comma-separated list. However, the default is to stop both. You can start slave threads with the `START SLAVE` statement.

Here's an example of both, run manually from the command-line with the `mysql` client:

Appendix A: SQL Statements & Functions, 129

STOP SLAVE

```
mysql -u myback_admin -p -e 'STOP SLAVE SQL_THREAD'

mysqldump --user=myback_admin --password=its_pwd \
        --all-databases --master-data --flush-logs \
        > /data/backups/backup.sql

mysql -u myback_admin -p -e 'START SLAVE SQL_THREAD'
```

When making a back-up of a slave, instead of totally stopping replication, you could just stop the SQL thread as show in this example. Using the `--flush-logs` option in conjunction with `--master-data`, the utility `mysqldump` will get a read lock on all tables so users cannot change any of the data until the back-up is finished. By stopping only the SQL thread, no changes to the data will be made by replication either. However, since the IO thread is still active, the slave will continue to receive updates from the master during the back-up. It will save these changes to the relay log as it does normally. Once the back-up is finished and you restart the SQL thread on the slave, the updates will be executed from the relay log.

Appendix B
MySQL Replication States

In order to be able to monitor effectively MySQL Replication, you need to know and understand the various states of the master and the slave. Server states can be displayed by using the SHOW PROCESSLIST statement on the master and the slave. You can also use the SHOW SLAVE STATUS on the slave, but that will only show you the slave's IO thread's state. Of course, that is the most important state to monitor.

Basically, in one or both of these SHOW statements, if replication is running, you will find a brief fragmented sentence describing what the master or slave is doing at the moment, or rather what each of the three replication threads is in. On the master, there is only the state of its binary log (i.e., the *Master BinLog Dump Thread State*) that relates to replication. On the slave, there is the IO thread (*Slave I/O Thread State*) for communications with the master related to replication, and there is the SQL thread (*Slave SQL Thread State*) which implements SQL statements related to replication of the master's databases. See Chapter 1, *MySQL Replication Process* for detailed descriptions of these threads, not their states. In this appendix, all replication states are grouped by the three types of replication threads just mentioned.

Appendix B MySQL Replication States

At the end of this appendix is an index listing the replication states to make it easier for you to find a particular in which you may encounter.

Using the SHOW PROCESSLIST on the master you should see at least one line of the results will be related to the replication activities for the user account associated with replication. However, this statement does not allow you to list only the replication process. For this, we can retrieve the process from the `processlist` table in the `information_schema` database.

Following the examples of this book, the user account is *replicant* on the master and shows as *system user* on the slave. In the Command column, on the master the value will be Binlog Dump, meaning a binary log thread; on the slave the command will be Connect. The results will also contain a field called State in which the state of the thread will be given. An example from a master follows, querying the `information_schema` database instead of using SHOW PROCESSLIST:

```
SELECT * FROM information_schema.processlist
WHERE user = 'replicant' \G

*************** 1. row ***************
     ID: 154766
   USER: replicant
   HOST: slave_host:46784
     DB: NULL
COMMAND: Binlog Dump
   TIME: 108903
  STATE: Has sent all binlog to slave;
         waiting for binlog to be updated
   INFO: NULL
```

The results here show that the master is waiting on user changes to hit the binary log.

Appendix B MySQL Replication States

Below is an example using the `SHOW PROCESSLIST` on the slave, with only the relevant rows shown:

```
SHOW PROCESSLIST \G
****************** 1. row ******************
     Id: 11
   User: system user
   Host:
     db: NULL
Command: Connect
   Time: 706340
  State: Waiting for master to send event
   Info: NULL
****************** 2. row ***************
     Id: 12
   User: system user
   Host:
     db: NULL
Command: Connect
   Time: 1
  State: Has read all relay log;
         waiting for the slave I/O thread to update it
   Info: NULL
```

These results show both threads, the I/O thread waiting on the master and the SQL thread waiting on the IO thread.

In addition to understanding these states, you may want to develop a script to check that replication is running on the slave and not stalled and to notify you if it's not running. Some ideas on how to do this may be found in Chapter 9, *Monitoring Replication*. Replication on MySQL is very stable, but if it does stop, it's very quiet about it. Fortunately, it's good about catching up rapidly once you restart it. However, it can catch up once you resolve the problem that stopped replication and restart the slave replicating. What follows is a list of replication states and explanations of each.

Appendix B MySQL Replication States

Master BinLog Dump Thread States

The following is a list of master server replication states that can be reported for binary log threads, known as *Binlog Dump Thread States*.

Has sent all binlog to slave; waiting for binlog to be updated

This is the most common status message you should see for a slave connection on the master. In this state, the master is basically doing nothing regarding replication at the moment. It has sent the slave all entries requested and is now waiting for another event to occur that will cause its binary log to be updated. Notice that it says that it is waiting for the binary log to be updated. It doesn't say that it's waiting for the databases to be updated. That's handled by a different component of MySQL. This thread lives only to provide information about the binary log to the slave.

Sending binlog event to slave

After the binary log has been updated, the master informs the slave that one or more new entries have been made. If the slave requests the entries, the master enters this state, indicating that it is in the process of sending a slave entries or information on pertinent database events. There are obviously other states in between, but they are so fast and short lived that they are not registered and therefore it is unlikely they will show up in the results of SHOW PROCESSLIST.

Master BinLog Dump Thread States

Finished reading one binlog; switching to next binlog

If a slave has been off-line for a while, the master may have flushed its logs in the interim. When this occurs, it will start a new log file, saving the previous ones. When a slave requests log entries that span more than one log file as the master switches from one file to the next, it enters this state.

Waiting to finalize termination

Once the master has completed the process of updating a slave, the master shows this state as its closing the binary log file and winding down the communication with the slave. When it is finished, the master will return to the first thread state in which it is waiting for more changes to the binary log.

Slave I/O Thread States

The IO thread is the thread which communicates with the master, receiving updates to the data and recording them in the relay log file. The following is a list of possible replication states related to IO thread states on the slave server:

Connecting to master

This state indicates that the slave I/O thread is attempting to connect to the master. If it can't connect, it may stay in this state for a while as it retries.

Checking master version

After the slave connects to the master, it compares versions of MySQL with the master to ensure compatibility. This is very quick.

Registering slave on master

After the slave connects to the master, it registers itself with the master as a replication slave server. During this process, it will be in this state. On the master side of the connection, the Binlog Dump state will be, "*Has sent all binlog to slave; waiting for binlog to be updated*," as described in the previous section.

Requesting binlog dump

When the slave has been informed of changes to the master binary log, it enters this state to request the new entries. Also, when it first connects to a server—either for the first time or after having been disconnected for a while—it enters this state briefly to request all entries since the last master binary log position that it gives the master. If no changes have occurred, none are returned. If there are new entries, the entries starting from the position given until the end of the master's binary log will be transmitted to the slave. On the master side, you will see the state, "*Sending binlog event to slave*" as a result of the request.

Waiting to reconnect after a failed binlog dump request

If the request for new entries mentioned in the previous state fails to be received from the master, the slave enters this state as it waits to be able to connect periodically to the master. This timeout period is configured using the `--master-connect-retry` and defaults to 60 seconds. The number of retries it will make can be found in the *master.info* file, as described in Chapter 1. Each time the slave attempts to reconnect, it will enter the next state.

Reconnecting after a failed binlog dump request

The slave failed to stay connected to the master while trying to retrieve entries to the master's binary log, as mentioned in the previous state description. This state indicates that the slave is trying to reconnect. If it fails again, it will go back to the previous state and wait to retry. By default, it will try 60 times before stopping. You can change the number of retries with the `--master-connect-retry` option for `mysqld`.

Slave I/O Thread States

Waiting for master update

This is initial state of the slave before it tries to connect to the master, before it enters the state, "*Connecting to master*".

Waiting for master to send event

This state is the most common one that you will see on the slave, unless your server is very busy. When in this state, the SQL thread is currently connected to the master and is waiting for the master to send it binary log updates. If there is no activity after a while, the connection will time out. The amount of seconds that will elapse before timeout is reached can be found in the global variable `slave_net_timeout` (previously `slave_read_timeout`) on the slave. A timeout is the same as a lost connection for the slave. Therefore, it will become active and attempt to reconnect to the master, then inquire about any changes to the master's binary log before entering this state again.

Queueing master event to the relay log

This state occurs when the slave I/O thread has received changes to the master's binary log from the master and is writing the SQL statements and the related information to the slave's relay log. Once it's done, the slave's SQL thread will read the relay log and execute the new SQL statements written to the log. On the SQL thread, this is the "*Reading event from the relay log*" state described below.

Slave I/O Thread States

Waiting to reconnect after a failed master event read

If the connection to the slave failed while reading an event (represented by an entry in the master's binary log), the slave will wait in this state for a certain amount of time before attempting to reconnect to the master. Prior to version 5.1.17 of MySQL, the amount of seconds that the slave will wait before retrying is found in the `master_connect_retry` variable on the slave. The new variable is `slave_net_timeout`. The default is 60 seconds. When the slave attempts to reconnect, it enters the next state.

Reconnecting after a failed master event read

This state occurs after the slave I/O thread lost its connection to the master while receiving an entry from the master binary log.

Waiting for the slave SQL thread to free enough relay log space

If the SQL thread isn't processing the entries in the relay log fast enough, and the backlog has caused the relay log files to become too large, the I/O thread will enter this state. In this state, it's waiting for the SQL thread to process enough of the entries in the relay log so that the I/O thread can delete some of the older content of the log. The maximum amount of space allocated for the relay log files is found in the `relay_log_space_limit` variable. The slave SQL thread automatically deletes relay log files. The `FLUSH LOGS` statement, though, causes the slave to rotate log files and to consider deleting old files.

Waiting for slave mutex on exit

When the I/O thread has been terminated, it enters this state as it closes. The term *mutex* stands for mutual exclusion. The SQL thread gets the mutex to prevent any other slave replication activities so that replication can be shut down without loss of data or file corruption.

Slave I/O Thread States

Slave SQL Thread States

The SQL thread is used for executing entries found in the relay log, SQL statements to update the data on the slave. A list of replication states that can be found on the slave server for SQL threads follows:

Has read all relay log; waiting for the slave I/O thread to update it

Because MySQL replication is so quick, you will see usually the slave's SQL thread in this state unless you have a very busy database system with data constantly being updated. This state indicates that the slave's SQL thread has read all of the entries in its relay log and has executed all of the SQL statements that it contains. It has no further updates to make to its databases and is waiting for the slave's I/O thread to add more entries to the relay log file. As mentioned in the similar state for the master, each thread acts somewhat independently and focuses only on the activities of its purview. Messages related to each thread's state reflect this.

Reading event from the relay log

When an entry has been made to the relay log by the slave's I/O thread, the slave's SQL thread enters this state. In this state it is reading the current relay log file starting from its last noted position and is executing the new SQL statements that it contains. Basically, in this state the SQL thread is busy updating the slave's databases.

Slave SQL Thread States

Waiting for slave mutex on exit

When the SQL thread has finished updating the slave's databases, it enters this state while it's closing the relay log file and terminating communications with the slave server. The SQL thread gets the mutex to prevent any other slave replication activities so that replication can be shut down without loss of data or file corruption. This is a very minimal state. However, if there is a problem with closing the relay log file or ending the activities with the slave server, the state is displayed so that you may know that the thread is locked. This could be caused by a table or log file being corrupted. If you see this state, you may want to run `myisamchk` or a similar utility, or the `REPAIR TABLE` statement on the tables that were accessed at the time of the lock up. You'll have to look in the relay log file and the error log file on the slave to determine which tables might need checking.

Waiting for the next event in relay log

The is the initial state of the SQL thread before it begins reading entries from the relay log, the state, "*Reading event from the relay log.*"

Making temp file

In this state, the thread is executing the SQL statement, `LOAD DATA INFILE` and thereby creating a temporary file related to this SQL statement. The file will, of course, contain the data it's loading. It will be located in the directory set by the `--slave-load-tmpdir` option. If this option isn't used, then the value of the `--tmpdir` option will be used in its stead.

Slave Connection Thread States

Besides the IO and SQL threads, you may find occasionally a connection thread related to replication on the slave in the results of the SHOW PROCESSLIST statement. They are related to activities outside of replication elements: the administrator starting and stopping the slave, changing master connection information, loading data from the master directly or from a data file on the slave. Below is a list and description of these connection thread states.

Changing master

This state indicates that the connection thread is executing the SQL statement, CHANGE MASTER TO on the slave.

Creating table from master dump

This state occurs when the slave is creating a table as a result of the SQL statement, CREATE TABLE found in a dump from the master. This state may also indicate that the SQL statements, LOAD TABLE FROM MASTER or LOAD DATA FROM MASTER are being executed. Both of these, though, are deprecated.

Killing slave

When the SQL statement, SLAVE STOP has been entered, while replication is being stopped, the slave will be in this state—usually, only for a short time.

Opening master dump table

After the state, "*Creating table from master dump*" ends, the connection thread will enter this state. It indicates that it's starting to execute the SQL statements in the dump file from the master. It is very briefly in this state before moving onto the next one.

Reading master dump table data

The slave connection thread will enter this state once a dump file from the master has been opened and execution of the SQL statements it contains has started. This is immediately after the state, "*Opening master dump table*". It indicates that is is reading a table of the dump file.

Rebuilding the index on master dump table

Once the slave has finished reading a table from a dump file from the master, it will rebuild an index related to the table. The slave connection thread will enter this state after the state, "*Reading master dump table data*".

Starting slave

This connection thread state indicates that the thread is starting the slave threads after having executed successfully the SQL statement, LOAD DATA FROM MASTER—which is deprecated.

Index of Replication States

Master BinLog Dump Thread States..135
   Has sent all binlog to slave; waiting for binlog to be updated..............135
   Sending binlog event to slave..135
   Finished reading one binlog; switching to next binlog...........................136
   Waiting to finalize termination...136
Slave I/O Thread States.. 137
   Connecting to master.. 137
   Checking master version... 137
   Registering slave on master...137
   Requesting binlog dump...137
   Waiting to reconnect after a failed binlog dump request.....................138
   Reconnecting after a failed binlog dump request...............................138
   Waiting for master update..139
   Waiting for master to send event...139
   Queueing master event to the relay log..139
   Waiting to reconnect after a failed master event read........................140
   Reconnecting after a failed master event read................................140
   Waiting for the slave SQL thread to free enough relay log space.........140
   Waiting for slave mutex on exit..141
Slave SQL Thread States.. 143
   Has read all relay log; waiting for the slave I/O thread to update it.....143
   Reading event from the relay log...143
   Waiting for slave mutex on exit..144
Slave Connection Thread States..145
   Changing master...145
   Creating table from master dump...145
   Killing slave..145
   Opening master dump table...146
   Reading master dump table data..146
   Rebuilding the index on master dump table....................................146
   Starting slave...146

Slave Connection Thread States

Appendix C
MySQL Daemon & Utilities

The MySQL daemon, `mysqld` has many options. Some of them are related particularly to MySQL Replication. Some others are related to aspects of MySQL that are not particular to replication but are still of concern to replication. For example, settings dealing with the binary log. This appendix contains a quick reference of these particular and related replication options for `mysqld`. It also contains reference information for the back-up utility, `mysqldump` and a couple of other utilities that are occasionally used by administrators concerned with replication.

Appendix CMySQL Daemon & Utilities

mysqld Daemon

When `mysqld` starts, various options can be used to alter the server's behavior. As a database administrator, if you're using replication, it may be useful to know what options exist related to replication. This section of this appendix lists `mysqld` options which are specifically and generally used with MySQL Replication.

Where and How to Use Options

Options may be given at the command-line when starting or restarting the server. However, it's common practice to enter them into the options file. On Unix-based systems, the main configuration file typically is `/etc/my.cnf`. For Windows systems, the main file is usually either `c:\systems\my.ini` or `c:\my.conf`. Options are entered on separate lines and follow a *variable=value* format. Some options are binary, and can be enabled by just including them with no value.

Within the options file, options are grouped under headings contained within square brackets. The `mysqld` daemon reads options from the configuration file under the headings of `[mysqld]` and `[server]` as it's started. For more recent versions of MySQL server, the group `[mysqld-5.0]` is also read. Groups are read in the order mentioned here and the last setting for an option read is the one used. However, options related to connection

mysqld Daemon

to the master are only read when replication is first set up. Subsequently, information files like the `master.info` file are used instead.

To get a list of options that `mysqld` is using on a particular server, enter the following line from the command-line. The results follow.

```
mysqld --print-defaults

mysqld would have been started with the following arguments:
  --datadir=/data/mysql/data
  --socket=/data/mysql/mysql.sock
  --server-id=2
  --report-host=home_svr
  --user=mysql
  --ft_min_word_len=3
  --default-character-set=utf8
  --log-bin=/data/logs/binary_log
  --log-bin-index=/data/logs/log-bin.index
  --log-error=/data/logs/error.log
  --relay-log=/data/logs/relay.log
  --relay-log-info-file=/data/logs/relay-log.info
  --relay-log-index=/data/logs/relay-log.index
  --slave-load-tmpdir=/data/mysql/tmp
  --skip-slave-start --skip_innodb
```

As the resulting message indicates, the `--print-defaults` options draws information from the options files and indicates the options and what their values would be if the MySQL server were restarted. However, if the options files were changed since MySQL was started, or if MySQL was started from the command-line, or with command-line options from a script on the server, this output will not reflect those options. Basically, the results of `--print-defaults` do not reflect the current settings, just the options it finds in the options files for the relevant server groups. To determine the current server options that have been used—other than the default options—while a server is running, from a Unix system you can enter the following command (sample results follow):

```
ps aux | grep mysql

mysql   22611   0.0  0.8   627504  17432 s000  S      2Jan10
4964:32.72 /usr/local/mysql/bin/mysqld
  --basedir=/usr/local/mysql
  --datadir=/data/mysql/data
  --user=mysql
  --log-error=/data/mysql/logs/mysqld.log
  --pid-file=/data/mysql/mysqld.pid
  --socket=/data/mysql/mysql.sock
```

If you see an option that you don't see in your default options file, it may be coming from a different options file. You may even be running a different installation of `mysqld` than you think. In such a situation, you would have to specify the path to the mysqld you want to use when starting the server.

What follows is an alphabetical listing of `mysqld` options either specifically for replication (e.g., `--replicate-ignore-db`) or generally used in relation to replication (e.g., `--bin-log-cache-size`). An explanation is given for each option of the purpose and use.

--abort-slave-event-count[=*number*]

This option is used by the MySQL test suite for testing and debugging replication. However, when used it limits the number of events from the relay log that are executed on the SQL thread. The default value is 0, which disables the option.

--auto_increment_increment[=*number*]

This option and the `--auto-increment-offset` option are used when replicating a master to a master server. This determines the amount by which an `AUTO_INCREMENT` column is increased which each new row inserted into any table in the system. By default, the variable associated with this option is set to 1. They can be set to a value from 1 to 65,535. If either option is set to 0, they both will be set back to 1. If either is set to a non-integer value, it will remain unchanged. If either is set to a negative value or a value in excess of 65,535, they both will then be set to 65,535. Don't use these options with MySQL Cluster as they cause problems.

--auto-increment-offset[=*number*]

Sets the starting number for `AUTO_INCREMENT` columns on all tables on the server. Each successive row inserted into tables will be incremented by the value of the `auto_increment_increment` system variable. If that variable is set to a number lower than the value set by this option, the value of the `auto_increment_offset` system variable (set by this option) will be ignored. See the description of the `--auto-increment-increment` option for more restrictions on this option.

--binlog-row-event-max-size=*number*

Use this option to give the maximum size in bytes of a row-based binary log event. As such, it's only available on servers which are capable of row-based replication. The default value is 1024; the value give should be in multiples of 256. This option is available as of version 5.1.5 of MySQL.

--binlog-do-db=*database*

This option limits the binary log to entries created by SQL statements executed for the database given, and only when it is the default database. If the user sets the default database to another database, but executes SQL statements affecting the database given with this option, those statements will not be written to the binary log. Additional databases may be specified with multiple instances of this option. Despite this option, though, `ALTER DATABASE`, `CREATE DATABASE`, and `DROP DATABASE` statements for the given database will be logged regardless of the default database setting.

--binlog-ignore-db=*database*

Omits entries from the binary log for SQL statements executed against the database given, but only when it is the default database. So when the user sets the default database to another database, but executes SQL statements affecting the database given with this

mysqld Daemon

option, those statements will be written to the binary log. Additional databases may be specified with multiple instances of this option. Despite this option, though, `ALTER DATABASE`, `CREATE DATABASE`, and `DROP DATABASE` statements for the given database will be logged regardless of the default database setting.

--binlog_cache_size=*number*

This option sets the size of the cache for temporarily holding SQL statements of a transactions to be written to the binary log. A binary log cache is established for each client, but only if the server is using transaction storage engines (e.g., InnoDB tables). Increasing the cache size can sometimes help with performance. Also for performance improvements, check the variable, `Binlog_cache_use` and the variable, `Binlog_cache_disk_use`.

--binlog-format={STATEMENT | ROW | MIXED}

This option is used to set the format to be used by the server when making binary log entries. There are three choices at this point: `STATEMENT`, `ROW`, or a combination called `MIXED`.

Statement-based formatting in the binary log basically logs SQL statements as they are given to the server. This was previously the default. It is generally a fine choice, but can be problematic when a statement involves databases other than the default one, the one set separately by the `USE` statement. Also, certain MySQL functions are deemed as unsafe with row-based formatting. For row-based formatting, if a statement includes changes to multiple tables, it will be separated into separate statements, affecting rows in only one table. This is generally safer, but can increase activity between the master and slave, slowing down replication on large servers. The mixed choice will cause the server to switch temporarily to row-based replication for a statement if the statement involves multiple tables and databases that may cause a problem with it being replicated properly on a slave, or if it uses a function designated by the developers as unsafe, one which will give a different results when executed on the master and by the SQL thread on the slave.

As of version 5.1.42 of MySQL the following functions are designated as unsafe for statement-based binary formatting: `GET_LOCK( )`, `IS_FREE_LOCK( )`, `IS_USED_LOCK( )`, `MASTER_POS_WAIT( )`, `RELEASE_LOCK( )`, `SLEEP( )`, `SYSDATE( )`, and `VERSION( )`.

The option, `--binlog-format` is available as of version 5.1.5 of MySQL—the variable equivalent (i.e., `binlog_format`) is available as of version 5.1.8. You cannot set this variable without `SUPER` privileges, even for a session. The choice of `MIXED` became available in version 5.1.8 of MySQL.

--disconnect-slave-event-count

This option is used by the MySQL test suite for testing and debugging replication.

--init-slave=*string*

Use this option on the server to specifies one or more SQL statements, all combined in a single string, that are to be executed by the slave each time its SQL thread starts.

--log-bin

Records database changes to a binary log to the filename given. If a filename isn't provided, the default name of host-bin.index will be used, where host is the host name of the server and index is a numeric count.

--log-bin-index=*name*

This option is used to specify the file path and name of the log-bin.index file. If you do not provide a file name, if will use the host name for the prefix. If you do not give a path, it will use data directory.

--log-bin-trust-function-creators[={0|1}]

By default, if binary logging is enabled, when creating a stored procedure, you have to state whether the function is deterministic and whether it will modify data. If this option is specified without a value or with a value of 1, this requirement is disabled. If set to 0, which is the default setting, the requirement is enabled.

--log-slave-updates

This option is used on a slave server to instruct it to write to its own binary log any updates to data made from SQL threads. The option requires that the --log-

`bin` option be used on the slave. With this method, it's possible to have a slave act as master to a slave under it.

--log-slow-slave-statements

This option requires slow query logging to be enabled (`--log-slow-queries`, `--slow_query_log` as of version 5.1.29 of MySQL). When it is, this option on the slave will log queries which took longer than the time allotted by the `long_query_time` variable on the slave. It's available as of version 5.1.21 of MySQL.

--log-warnings[=*level*]

Activates logging of warning messages. Prior to version 4.0 of MySQL, this option was invoked with the `--warnings` option. After version 4.1.2, this option is enabled by default and can be disabled with the `--skip-log-warnings` option.

--master-connect-retry=*seconds*

Sets the number of seconds that a slave thread may sleep before trying to reconnect to the master. The default is 60 seconds. This value is also included in the master.info file. If that file exists and is accessible, the value contained in it will override this option.

--master-host=*host*

This option is superseded by the same information in the master.info file and is necessary for replication. It that file doesn't exist or is inaccessible, this option may be used to set the host name or IP address of the master server.

--master-info-file=*file*

Sets the name of the master information file. This file is described in detail in Chapter 1, *MySQL Replication Process*. By default, this file is named master.info and is located in the data directory of MySQL.

--master-password=*password*

If the `master.info` file doesn't exist or is inaccessible, this option may be used to set the password used by the slave thread for accessing the master server.

--master-port=*port*

Sets the port number on which the master will listen for replication. By default, it's 3306. The value for this variable in the master.info file, if available, will override this option.

--master-retry-count=*count*

Specifies the number of times the slave should try to connect to the master if attempts fail. The default value is 86400. The interval between retries is set by the option `--master-connect-retry`. Retries are initiated when the slave connection times out for the amount of time set with the `--slave-net-timeout` option.

--master-ssl

Specifies that an SSL connection for the slave with the master should be used. Requires the server to have SSL enabled.

--master-ssl-ca=*file*

Specifies the name of the file (i.e., the pem file) containing a list of trusted SSL Ca's for slave connections to the master.

--master-ssl-capath=*directory*

Specifies the path to the trusted certificates file (i.e., the pem file) for slave connections to the master.

--master-ssl-cert=*file*

Specifies the name of the SSL certificate file to use for SSL connections for slave connections to the master.

--master-ssl-cipher=*cipher_list*

Gives a list of ciphers that may be used for SSL encryption for slave connections to the master.

--master-ssl-key=*file*

Specifies the SSL key file to use for secure connections for slave connections to the master.

--master-user=*user*

Sets the name of the user account that the slave thread uses to connect to the master server for replication. The user given must have REPLICATION SLAVE privilege on the master. This option is overridden by the master.info file.

--max-binlog-size=*size*

This option is useful in reducing the size of the binary log files. When a binary log file reaches the maximum size in bytes that you set with this option, it rotate the binary log files to start a new one. The maximum size is the default of 1GB. Incidentally, the log rotation won't begin until the current transactions are completed.

--max-relay-log-size=*size*

This option is useful in reducing the size of the relay log files on a slave server. When a relay log file reaches the maximum size in bytes that you set with this option, it rotate the relay log files to start a new one. The maximum size is 1GB. If you set this option to a value of 0, though, it instructs the server to use the value set with the `--max-binlog-size` option.

--read-only

This option prevents users from adding, changing, or deleting data on the server, except for users with SUPER privileges. The other exception is that updates from slave threads are allowed. This option does not carry over from a master to its slaves. It can be set on slaves independently from the master and may be useful to do so to keep slaves synchronized properly.

--relay-log=*file*

Sets the root name of the relay log file. By default, it's slave_host_name-relay-bin. MySQL will rotate the log files and append a suffix to the file name given with this option. The suffix is generally a seven digit number, counting from 0000001.

--relay-log-index=*file*

Sets the name of the relay log index file. By default, it's `slave_host_name-relay-bin.index`.

--relay-log-info-file=*file*

Sets the name of the file that the slave will use to record information related to the relay log. By default, it's `relay-log.info` and is located in the data directory of MySQL.

--relay-log-purge={0|1}

This option is used to make the server automatically purge relay logs when it determines they are no longer necessary. The default value of 1 enables it; a value of 0 disables it.

--relay-log-space-limit=*size*

Use this option to set the maximum amount of space in bytes that may be used by all relay logs on a slave.

mysqld Daemon

--replicate-do-db=*database*

Tells the slave thread to limit replication to SQL statements executed against the database given, and only when it is the default database. When the user sets the default database to another database, but executes SQL statements affecting the database given with this option, those statements will not be replicated. Additional databases may be specified with multiple instances of this option.

--replicate-do-table=*database.table*

Tells the slave thread to limit replication to SQL statements executed against the table given. Additional tables may be specified with multiple instances of this option.

--replicate-ignore-db=*database*

Skips replication for SQL statements executed against the database given, but only when it is the default database. So when the user sets the default database to another database, but executes SQL statements affecting the database given with this option, those statements will be replicated. Additional databases may be specified with multiple instances of this option.

--replicate-ignore-table=*database.table*

Omits replication of SQL statements executed against the table given. Additional tables may be specified with multiple instances of this option.

--replicate-rewrite-db="*database*->*database*"

Tells the slave to change the database with the first name to have the second name (the name after the ->), but only when the default database on the master is set to the first database.

--replicate-same-server-id

If this option is set to 1, entries in the binary log with the same server-id as the slave will be replicated. This potentially can cause an infinite loop of replication, so it shouldn't be implemented unless necessary and then only for a limited time and purpose. This option is set to 0 by default and is used on the slave server. The option is ignored if `--log-slave-updates` is enabled.

--replicate-wild-do-table=*database.table*

This option is similar to `--replicate-do-table` except that you may give wildcards (% or _) for the database and table names. For instance, to match all tables that start with the name `clients`, you would give a value of `clients%`. To literally give a percent-sign or an underscore, escape the character with a preceding backslash (i.e., \% and _). Additional tables may be specified with multiple instances of this option.

--replicate-wild-ignore-table=*database.table*

This option is similar to `--replicate-ignore-table` except that you may give wildcards (% or _) for the database and table names. For instance, to match all tables that start with the name `clients`, you would give a value of `clients%`. To literally give a percent-sign or an underscore, escape the character with a preceding backslash (i.e., `\%` and `\_`). Additional tables may be specified with multiple instances of this option.

--report-host=*host*

Because the master cannot always ascertain the slave's host name or IP address, use this option to have the slave register with the master and report its host name or IP address. This information will be returned when `SHOW SLAVE HOSTS` is executed on the master.

--report-password=*password*

Sets the password used by the slave to register with the master. If the `--show-slave-auth-info` option is enabled, this information will be returned when `SHOW SLAVE HOSTS` is executed on the master.

--report-port=*port*

Sets the port used by the slave to communicate with the master. This option should be employed only when a special port is being used or if the server has special tunneling requirements.

--report-user=*user*

Sets the user name used by the slave to register with the master. If the `--show-slave-auth-info` option is enabled, this information will be returned when `SHOW SLAVE HOSTS` is executed on the master.

--server-id=*number*

Sets the local server's server identifier. It must be used on the master as well as each slave, must be unique for each server, and should be set in the options file.

--show-slave-auth-info

This option causes the SQL statement SHOW SLAVE HOSTS to reveal the slave's user name and password, if the slave was started with the --report-user and the --report-password options.

--skip-slave-start

If this option is enabled, the master server won't automatically start the slaves when it's restarted. Instead, you will have to enter the START SLAVE statement on each slave to start it.

--slave-compressed-protocol={0|1}

If set to 1, this option instructs the slave to compress data passed between it and the master, if they support compression. The default is 0.

--slave-load-tmpdir=*directory*

Specifies the directory where the slave stores temporary files used by the LOAD DATA INFILE statement.

--slave-net-timeout=seconds

Specifies the number of seconds before a slave connection times out and the slave attempts to reconnect. See the options `--master-connect-retry` and `--master-retry-count`, as they related to this option.

--slave-skip-errors={error_code[, error_code, ...]|all}

By default, replication stops on the slave when an error occurs. This option instructs the slave not to terminate replication for specific errors. Error numbers for the errors should be given in a comma-separated list. You may specify all errors by giving the value of all. This option generally should not be used, and the value of all in particular should probably never be used.

--slave-transaction-retries=number

Specifies the number of times the slave should try to execute a transaction before returning an error if the transaction fails because of problems related to InnoDB or NDB settings. For InnoDB, this applies if there is a deadlock or if the transaction takes more time than is allowed by `innodb_lock_wait_timeout`. For NDB, this applies if the transaction takes more time than is allowed by `TransactionDeadlockDetectionTimeout` or `TransactionInactiveTimeout`. The default value of this option is 10.

--sporadic-binlog-dump-fail

This option is used by the MySQL test suite for testing and debugging replication.

--sql-slave-skip-counter

When the slave begins to re-execute commands that the master executed, this option causes the slave to skip the first number events from the master's log.

--sync-binlog=*number*

If this option is set to a value of 1, the server will synchronize every write to the binary log to the disk. The default value of 0 disables this feature.

mysqld Daemon

mysql_fix_privilege_tables

At various points the user security database `mysql` underwent some changes: the complexity of the passwords were changed, more privileges were added, etc. To make upgrading an existing database easier, you can use this utility to implement the changes between versions. Be sure to restart the MySQL server when you have finished running this utility for the changes to take effect. As of version 5.0.19 of MySQL, this utility has been replaced by `mysql_upgrade`. It performs the same functions and has other capabilities.

There are only two options for the program, `mysql_fix_privilege_tables`. One is `--password`, in which the root password is given. The other option is `--verbose`. It's used to display more information when running this utility.

On Windows systems this program is not available. However, there is an SQL file, `mysql_fix_privilege_tables.sql` which may be run with the `mysql` client as `root` to perform the same tasks. The SQL file is located either in the *scripts* or the *share* directory where MySQL is installed.

mysql_fix_privilege_tables

mysqldump

This utility exports MySQL data and table structures. Typically, you would use this utility to make back-ups of databases or to copy databases from one server to another. The MySQL server must be active when running it. For consistency of data between tables, the tables should be locked. Below are three syntaxes for this utility:

```
mysqldump [options] --all-databases
mysqldump [options] --databases database [database ...]
mysqldump [options] database [table]
```

The first method shown is a simple one used to make a back-up of all databases for the server. The second method backs up specific databases, named in a space-separated list, including all tables in each database. The third method backs up specific tables of a specific database. For examples of these different syntaxes and for information on making a back-up for replication with mysqldump, see Chapter 4, *Copying Initial Data*. For information on restoring a back-up made with mysqldump, see Chapter 8, *Restoring a Back-up*.

The contents of the dump file can be determined by the options chosen. The following is an alphabetical list of options that an administrator might consider when using replication, along with a brief explanation of each. This is not a complete list of all options available.

--add-drop-database

Adds a `DROP DATABASE` statement followed by a `CREATE DATABASE` statement to the dump file for each database. When the dump file is used to restore databases, this will replace the existing databases and data. When first setting up a slave, this may be the best choice, of course.

--add-drop-table

Adds a `DROP TABLE` statement to the export file before each set of `INSERT` statements for each table. When the dump file is used to restore tables, this option will delete the existing tables and data before loading the back-up copies.

--add-locks

Adds a `LOCK` statement before each set of `INSERT` statements and an `UNLOCK` after each set. When making a back-up, this will give you consistency of data for each table, but not necessarily across databases. So if two tables have a logical relationship to each other and a user changes one, before a back-up starts and the other after it finishes, there may be an inconsistency of the data in the dump file. It might be better to use `--flush-logs`, especially for replication related back-ups.

--all, -a

Includes all MySQL-specific statements in the export file. This option is deprecated as of version 4.1.2 of MySQL. It is replaced with the `--create-options` option.

--all-databases, -A

This `mysqldump` option instructs the utility to export all databases on the server. If you want to back-up only certain databases, use the `--databases` option. To back-up all databases except for certain tables, use `--all-databases` with `--ignore-table` option.

--compact

Omits comments from the dump file to make the file more compact. It also calls the `--skip-add-drop-table`, `--skip-add-locks`, `--skip-disable-keys`, and `--skip-set-charset` options. Don't confuse this option with `-compress`. Before version 5.1.2, this option did not work with databases that contained views.

--complete-insert, -c

Generates complete `INSERT` statements in the export file. This uses the syntax of the `INSERT` statement, which includes the `SET` keyword and the column name for each value.

--compress, -C

This option tells the utility to compresses data passed between the utility and the server, if compression is supported by the server and your build of `mysqldump`.

--create-options

This says to include all MySQL-specific table options with `CREATE TABLE` statements in the dump file.

--databases, -B

Use this to name more than one database to export. Table names may not be given with this option unless using the `--tables` option.

```
mysqldump -u russell -p --flush-logs --databases \
    > /home/russell/backup.sql
```

--delete-master-logs

Instructs the utility to lock all tables on all servers and then to delete the binary logs of a master replication server after completing the export. Using this option also invokes the `--master-data` option.

--events, -E

Use this option if you want to include events from the databases. This option is available as of version 5.1.8.

--extended-insert, -e

Bundles `INSERT` statements together for each table in the export file to make the export faster. Otherwise a separate `INSERT` statement for each row of each table will be placed in the dump file.

--first-slave

Locks all tables on all servers. This option has been deprecated and replaced with `--lock-all-tables`.

--flush-logs, -F

This option flushes all logs on the server before the export begins. It requires the user to have `RELOAD` privilege on the server. If this option is used with --

all-databases, the logs are flushed before each database is exported. To have the logs flushed once before the export starts and not for each database, use the `--lock-all-tables` or `--master-data` with this option.

--flush-privileges

This option flushes all privileges by executing the `FLUSH PRIVILEGES` statement after exporting the `mysql` database. It was added as of version 5.1.12.

--host=*host*, -h *host*

This specifies the name or IP address of the server for connection. The localhost is the default. The user and host combination and related privileges will need to be set on the server.

--ignore-table=*database.table*

Use this option to tell mysqldump not to export a particular table of a given database. For more than one table, enter this option multiple times with one database and table combination for each. You can also use this option to avoid exporting views: just give the view name instead of the table name.

--lock-tables, -l

This option tells the utility to get a `READ LOCK` on all tables of each database before exporting the database, but not all databases at the same time. It will lock a database before it begins to dump it. It will release the lock on the database before locking and dumping the next database. This option is typically used with MyISAM tables. For transactional storage engines, use `--single-transaction` instead. However, for consistency in data across databases, consider using `--lock-all-databases`.

--lock-all-tables, -x

This option will have mysqldump lock all tables on all databases, a global read lock while exporting. It will undo the `--single-transaction` option in `mysqldump`.

--log-error=*logfile*

Writes errors and warning messages to the file named. The file path may be included. It's available as of version 5.1.18.

--master-data=*value*

This option has mysqldump include CHANGE MASTER TO statements in the dump file. It includes two lines with the statements: one for the name of the current binary log file on the master and master's position in the log file. The option requires RELOAD privilege. It typically will disable `--lock-tables` and `--lock-all-tables`.

--no-autocommit

Adds SET AUTOCOMMIT=0: before each INSERT statement, and a COMMIT; statement after each INSERT statement.

--no-create-db, -n

Instructs the utility not to add `CREATE DATABASE` statements to the export file when the `--all-databases` option or the `--databases` option is used.

--no-create-info, -t

Instructs the utility not to add `CREATE TABLE` statements to the export file.

--opt

This option is a combination of several commonly used options: `--add-drop-table`, `--add-locks`, `--create-options` (or `--all` instead before version 4.1.2), `--disable-keys`, `--extended-insert`, `--lock-tables`, `--quick`, and `--set-charset`. As of version 4.1, the `--opt` option is enabled by default. Use `--skip-opt` to disable it for users with limited access.

--order-by-primary

Sorts rows of tables by their primary key or first index. It slows down the back-up process, though.

--password[=*password*], -p[*password*]

Provides the password to pass to the server. A space is not permitted after `-p` if the password is given. If the password is not given when using the `-p` option, the user will be prompted for one.

--port=*port*, -P *port*

Specifies the port number to use for connecting to the server. A space is expected before the port number when using the -P form of the option.

--protocol=*protocol*

Used to specify the type of protocol to use for connecting to the server. The choices are TCP, SOCKET, PIPE, and MEMORY.

--quick, -q

Instructs the utility not to buffer data into a complete results set before exporting. Instead, data is exported one row at a time directly to the export file.

--replace

Puts REPLACE statements into the dump file instead of INSERT statements. This was added as of version 5.1.3.

--result-file=*filename*, -r *filename*, > *filename*

Provides the path and the name of the file to which data should be exported. Use the --result-file option on Windows systems to prevent new-line characters (\n) from being converted to carriage-return and new-line characters (\r\n).

--routines, -R

Dumps stored procedures and functions. This option was added as of version 5.1.2. It requires SELECT privilege in the proc table of the mysql database. The statements written to the dump file related to these routines do not include timestamps, so the current time will be used when restoring instead.

--single-transaction

Executes a `BEGIN` statement before exporting to help achieve data consistency with the back-up. It's effective only on transactional storage engines.

--skip-opt

Disables the `--opt` option.

--ssl

Specifies that secure SSL connections should be used. Requires the server to have SSL enabled. If this option is enabled on the utility by default, use `--skip-ssl` to disable it.

--ssl-ca=*pem_file*

Specifies the name of the file (i.e., the `pem` file) containing a list of trusted SSL CAs.

--ssl-capath=*path*

Specifies the path to the trusted certificates file (i.e., the pem file).

--ssl-cert=*filename*

Specifies the name of the SSL certificate file to use for SSL connections.

--ssl-cipher=*ciphers*
Gives a list of ciphers that may be used for SSL encryption

--ssl-key=*filename*
Specifies the SSL key file to use for secure connections.

--ssl-verify-server-cert
Verifies the client's certificate against the server's certificate for the client at start-up. It is available as of version 5.1.11.

--socket=*filename*, -S *filename*
Provides the name of the server's socket file on Unix type system, or the named pipe on Windows systems.

--tables
Specifies tables to dump. All names after the `--tables` option are treated as table names and not as database names.

--triggers
Includes triggers in dump files. This option is the default. Use `--skip-triggers` to disable it.

--tz-utc
Adds `SET TIME_ZONE='+00:00';` to the dump file so that the dump files may be restored on a server in a different time zone and not cause inconsistencies with

mysqldump

`TIMESTAMP` columns. This option is available as of version 5.1.2 and enabled by default. Use `--skip-tz-utc` to disable it.

--user=*user*, -u user

Specifies the username for connecting to the server. A space is expected after the `-u` option. If the `-u` version of this option is used and the user name is not given, the current system user is assumed.

mysqldump

mysql_upgrade

Use this utility after upgrading to a new version of MySQL. It updates the `mysql` database for new privileges and other factors. It also checks all tables in all databases for version incompatibilities and corrects them if possible. It then tags the tables for the new version so that they won't be checked again. It notes the version number in the `mysql_upgrade_info` file located in the data directory. This utility replaces `mysql_fix_privilege_tables`. Below are options available for this utility, listed alphabetically:

--basedir=*path*

Specifies the base directory of the MySQL server.

--datadir=*path*

Specifies the data directory of the MySQL server.

--force

Forces the utility to check tables despite the `mysql_upgrade_info` file indicating that the tables are marked the same as the version noted in that file.

--password=*password*, -p *password*

Provides the password of the user logging into the server.

--user=*user*, -u *user*

Provides the user name for logging in to the server. If the option is not given, `root` is assumed by default.

mysql_upgrade

Index

Automating Back-ups	77
CHANGE MASTER TO	41, 42, 113, 126
Copying of Data	54
Error Log	25
error.log	25
expire_logs_days	118
FLUSH LOGS	17, 140
GRANT OPTION	29
InnoDB	38, 54
LAVE throw	74
LIMIT clause	122
LOAD DATA FROM MASTER	53, 114
LOAD DATA FROM MASTER	54
LOAD DATA INFILE	40, 41
LOAD TABLE...FROM MASTER	115, 116
log-bin	37, 40, 118
log-error	40, 178
master_connect_retry	140
MASTER_LOG_FILE	115, 128
MASTER_LOG_POS	115, 128
MASTER_POS_WAIT( )	111, 116
MASTER_SSL	114
master-connect-retry	138
master.info	17, 41, 42, 74, 113, 114, 119, 138
max_binlog_size	17
max_relay_log_size	17
myisamchk	144
mysql_fix_privilege_tables	171
mysql_upgrade	185
mysqladmin	8
mysqlbinlog	10, 123
mysqld	151
mysqldump	173
net_read_timeout	115
net_write_timeout	115
Privilege, RELOAD	176, 178
Privilege, REPLICATE CLIENT	30
Privilege, REPLICATE SLAVE	30

Privilege, SUPER	61, 73, 121
PURGE MASTER LOGS	117, 124
Relay_Log_File	23
RELAY_LOG_FILE	81
Relay_Log_Pos	23
RELAY_LOG_POS	81
relay_log_space_limit	140
relay-log-info-file	40
relay-log.info	22
RELOAD	176, 178
REPAIR TABLE	144
REPLICATE CLIENT	30
REPLICATE SLAVE	30
RESET MASTER	118, 119
RESET SLAVE	119, 127
SET	12
SET GLOBAL SQL_SLAVE_SKIP_COUNTER	120
SET SQL_LOG_BIN	121
SHOW BINARY LOGS	118
SHOW BINLOG EVENTS	121
SHOW MASTER LOGS	13, 118, 122, 123
SHOW MASTER STATUS	30, 113, 124
SHOW PROCESSLIST	131, 135
SHOW SLAVE HOSTS	125
SHOW SLAVE STATUS	20, 23, 30, 113, 114, 118, 126, 129
SHOW SLAVE STATUS \G	62
SHOW SLAVE STATUS, we	21
Slave Status	20
slave_net_timeout	139
slave_read_timeout	139
slave-load-tmpdir	40, 41
slave-load-tmpdir	144
START SLAVE	62, 81, 112, 128, 129
STOP SLAVE	74, 81, 112, 129
SUPER	61, 73, 121
Syntax:	114, 116
TIMESTAMP	12
tmpdir	40, 41
tmpdir	144
UNLOCK TABLES	57
UNTIL	81, 128
user account, set up	29
users table	49

--abort-slave-event-count[=number] ... 154
--add-drop-database ... 174
--add-drop-table ... 174
--add-locks ... 174
--all ... 174
--all-databases ... 175
--auto_increment_increment ... 154
--auto-increment-offset ... 154
--basedir ... 185
--binlog_cache_size ... 156
--binlog-do-db ... 155
--binlog-format={STATEMENT | ROW | MIXED} ... 156
--binlog-ignore-db ... 155
--binlog-row-event-max-size ... 155
--compact ... 175
--complete-insert ... 175
--compress ... 175
--create-options ... 175
--databases ... 176
--datadir ... 185
--delete-master-logs ... 176
--disconnect-slave-event-count ... 157
--events ... 176
--extended-insert ... 48, 176, 179
--first-slave ... 176
--flush-logs ... 176
--flush-privileges ... 177
--force ... 185
--host ... 177
--ignore-table ... 49, 177
--init-slave ... 158
--lock-all-tables ... 178
--lock-tables ... 177-179
--log-bin ... 38, 118, 158
--log-bin-index ... 158
--log-bin-trust-function-creators ... 158
--log-slave-updates ... 158
--log-slow-slave-statements ... 159
--log-warnings ... 159
--master-connect-retry ... 138, 159
--master-data ... 49, 61, 176, 178
--master-host ... 160
--master-info-file ... 160

--master-password ... 160
--master-port ... 160
--master-retry-count ... 160
--master-ssl ... 161
--master-ssl-ca ... 161
--master-ssl-capath ... 161
--master-ssl-cert ... 161
--master-ssl-cipher ... 161
--master-ssl-key ... 161
--master-user ... 162
--max-binlog-size ... 162
--max-relay-log-size ... 162
--no-autocommit ... 178
--no-create-db ... 179
--no-create-info ... 179
--opt ... 179, 181
--order-by-primary ... 179
--password ... 179, 185
--port ... 180
--protocol ... 180
--quick ... 180
--read-only ... 162
--relay-log ... 163
--relay-log-index ... 163
--relay-log-info-file ... 163
--relay-log-purge ... 163
--relay-log-space-limit ... 163
--replace ... 180
--replicate-do-db ... 164
--replicate-do-table ... 164
--replicate-ignore-db ... 164
--replicate-ignore-table ... 164
--replicate-rewrite-db ... 165
--replicate-same-server-id ... 165
--replicate-wild-do-table ... 165
--replicate-wild-ignore-table ... 165
--report-host ... 166
--report-host=slave ... 125
--report-password ... 166
--report-port ... 166
--report-user ... 166
--result-file ... 180
--routines ... 180

--server-id 167
--show-slave-auth-info 167
--single-transaction 181
--skip-opt 179, 181
--skip-slave-start 82, 167
--slave-compressed-protocol 167
--slave-load-tmpdir 167
--slave-net-timeout 168
--slave-skip-errors 168
--slave-transaction-retries 168
--socket 182
--sporadic-binlog-dump-fail 168
--sql-slave-skip-counter 169
--ssl 181
--ssl-ca 181
--ssl-capath 181
--ssl-cert 181
--ssl-cipher 182
--ssl-key 182
--ssl-verify-server-cert 182
--sync-binlog 169
--tables 182
--triggers 182
--tz-utc 182
--user 183, 185

Made in the USA
Lexington, KY
04 October 2012